ALL INCOMPLETE

Stefano Harney and Fred Moten

Foreword by Denise Ferreira da Silva
Photos and Afterword by Zun Lee

Minor Compositions 2021

All Incomplete
Stefano Harney and Fred Moten

ISBN 978-1-57027-378-0

Cover image by Zun Lee
Cover design by Haduhi Szukis
Edited by Stevphen Shukaitis
Interior design by Margaret Killjoy

All primary photography by Zun Lee (http://www.zunlee.com)

Released by Minor Compositions 2021
Colchester / New York / Port Watson

Minor Compositions is a series of interventions & provocations drawing from autonomous politics, avant-garde aesthetics, and the revolutions of everyday life.

Minor Compositions is an imprint of Autonomedia
www.minorcompositions.info | minorcompositions@gmail.com

Distributed by Autonomedia
PO Box 568 Williamsburgh Station
Brooklyn, NY 11211

www.autonomedia.org
info@autonomedia.org

CONTENTS

Acknowledgments 1
Foreword 5
    Denise Ferreira da Silva
The Theft of Assembly 13
We Want a Precedent 23
Usufruct and Use 27
Leave Our Mikes Alone 37
Unwatchable, Unwatchable 51
Al-Khwāriddim 55
A Partial Education 61
Indent 79
Against Management 89
Base Faith 113
Plantocracy and Communism 119
Who Determines if Something is Habitable? 131
Black (Ante)Heroism 137
Suicide as a Class 145
The Gift of Corruption 155
Home is Where We Displace our Selves 169
    Zun Lee
Endnotes 173

Acknowledgments

We would like to acknowledge BAK, Duke University Press, *e-flux*, M.I.T. Press, Museo Nacional Centro de Arte Reina Sofía, The New Museum, Routledge, Rutgers University Press, The University of Minnesota Press and Verso. "Suicide as a Class" was originally commissioned and published as part of *Return to the Source* (returntothesource.info) in September 2020.

for Manolo Callahan
(to renew our habits of assembly)

FOREWORD

Denise Ferreira da Silva

EVERY DECISION ALWAYS INCLUDES A CHOICE OF ONE THING AMONG OTHERS; A choice which is always also of the lesser because no one thing can meet all demands of what is called desire. Or, perhaps, it is the lesser because what we call desire is but the presence of a demand to choose, to decide, to pick one and only one, and go your merry way. Either way, the algorithm, the formal deciding tools of logistical capital fails where it has to work with more than what is adequate for it to do its thing, to choose, to decide. When the input does not match the data, the process stalls. An input, any input is always less than a thing. It is never raw material; it is never just something. Input is data, it has a form and a purpose. It is always ready to be in relation, to make a connection. Which means also that, for it to work, for the algorithm to do its thing, the input it needs to fit as part in the structure and be able to facilitate the procedure it is submitted to, it needs to be processable. This is way an input cannot be a thing. It is always an object.

Despite of what Heidegger may say it is, the thing does not exist exclusively for the existential thing. Nor does Descartes' exercise on mental fitness immediately and irrevocability renders a thing *res extensa*. More along the lines of what Kant realized, the thing exceeds whatever can be apprehended as form, as object or data. As such, a thing always mismatches the structure (and do so because it extends beyond the boundaries of the input because it does not find its proper place within them) and slows the procedure to halt (as what in it is in excess of the input, what in it is not data overflows of the possibilities for what is to come). That which in the thing exceeds the parameters of form and efficacy can never enter in the process, unless it is already deject, reject, or just as well as dead.

No-thing is a thing as much as anything is every-thing. What is the thing then? A thing is but this incomprehensible incompleteness, which is also Stefano Harney and Fred Moten generously offer to our attention. Incomprehensible incompleteness is then not so much the name for something or a somewhere from where resistance is attempted. Against scarcity, and the juridical and ethical terms with which it has dressed up the subjects of property, sovereignty, or desire, *res imperfectum* as *res improprium* is just another name for the material capacity (the power of matter) which is perhaps what Stefano Harney and Fred Moten calls jus generativity, the one for which I propose generosity as principle.

I.

Incomprehension, as it is intended in this thank you note to Stefano and Fred, accentuates this failing because it recalls how formality and efficacy both request and give completeness.

That which does not exhibit either cannot be seen as total, finalized, absolute, or perfect. It is not then comprehensible: it does not explain (account for) itself, either all of its various parts or as a whole. That which does not exhibit, has proper forms, and follows the straight line is incomplete and as such it is not a body (for the idea of a body gives the whole for which all parts are account) and it is not world (for the idea of world gives a part that can account for the whole). Improper structures and warped procedures are not comprehensible even in the very statement – Gödel's theorems – that ascertain the incompleteness of the prevailing mode of thinking. And, as such, because it has no structure (as body or world or a system), no part (organ, subjectivity or axiom), and no movement (blood circulation, historicity, or reasoning). These are of course differing kinds of forms, parts, and movements; however, all three, when combined obtains the idea of development, in the sense that the movement, through which the parts are connected, sustains or brings the whole to completion. Without structure and its parts how are you to know what to improve? What needs improvement? What has already achieved it? Without a procedure and its result how does the whole subsist? How do the parts combine to produce an effect? What keeps on going on its own? And how? How can improvement take place without a what and a how?

Without structure and procedure, there is no resistance, only existents without goals, elements without purpose, and intraferences without higher or lower motives. Or as reading *All Incomplete* helps us to recall, all there is in bare incomprehensible incompleteness or compliance to deep implication, which is the same thing as existential ac-complicity. In impropriety, whether as the breaking of a rule or the violation of a principle, there is no position or pre-occupation from which to resist transformation (that is, corruption, which is the becoming implicated in the constitution of everything), to insist in remaining what it has never being or will become, namely complete. This is the gift. In logisticality, it is not so much the where and how and to what end of the movement – all of which concern the improvement of the flow – but instead it is the that after that, which would not necessarily or even accidentally have to follow from that which preceded or would not necessarily have to precede that which followed. Un-prehensible, undercommons sociality, or black study, might just take us along, without plot or plan, as/in earthly existence, that is, guided but by the jus generativity that prevails under existence's unbounded generosity. Thank you Stefano and Fred!

II.

The paradox of political corruption is that it is the modality through which brutal institutionality is maintained. The paradox of biosocial corruption is that it constitutes the militant preservation of a general, generative capacity to differ and diffuse. These paradoxes combine to gild the edge of corruption, turn it towards a gift, which was already double-edged, which we might wear, or don, as if it were the very fabric of our skin.

Of all on that the juridic and the scientific depend and append, property is perhaps the most obvious and the least straightforward. It is obvious in the sense that it is something that is had but it is not straightforward because this having can take the form of an attribute (a quality) or an article (a target, an object, or a goal). Un-com-prehensible incompleteness misses both, as it signals how all that exists has as missing that part through which each and everything exists with/as/in something else.

Propriety, as referring to a rule or a principle, necessarily recalls these two aspects of what is had, and undoing so, it hopelessly brings up that which has the having. Improvement, Harney and Moten offer, is very much contingent on that figure – Man, Subject, Human, or Humanity – whose parts proceed in such a way as to render it not only the embodiment of perfection, but the body/mind that is capable of bringing other existing things to perfection. That thing with property, that is, the juridic-economic figure taking precedence over any alternative description of existence is not, however, self-sufficient. For it has always depended on colonial juridic-economic architectures and the racial ethic-symbolic arsenal, improvement itself, the quality and capacity said to distinguish has also always being contingent upon our impropriety.

Res improprium, that which a thing, any thing, every thing has become when preposed, that is, when considered before (temporally and spatially) the *res proprium* (the Cartesian thing as presented by John Locke and Adam Smith), it turns out, might be the only acceptable descriptor for the ultimate condition of possibility for capital accumulation. For improvement/usufruct – the Subject's quality and capacity – to be possible it is required that impropriety be necessary (as an quality of exclusive to its other), and, the other way around, that is, for it to be possible it is required that propriety be necessary (as quality intrinsic to the transparent I). Only the proper thing, the one that has and knows perfection, is capable of actualizing perfection in/as world – Stefano and Fred remind us then why we'd better watch out of it, both perfection (as the threat) and world (to be rescued from it). However, because its propriety has been articulated in an intrinsic comparison, in contradiction with everything else's exclusive impropriety, because it makes no sense without it, *res proprium* cannot improve all its parts; if it does so, it will transform its trajectory into an eschatology.

No equivalence here. *Res proprium* is not the condition for the articulation of what has been named *improprium* in contradistinction with it. For the gift, of which Harney and Moten remind us, is impropriety, that is, this consistent and continuous re/de/generation, our corruption, "generative capacity to differ and diffuse." Unbounded impropriety of things is that which re/de/generates through a kink the very computation designed for improving (on) them.

III.

If their logistics both assumes and dictates that the shortest distance between two points is a straight line, what if our logisticality, before and against both assumption and dictation, improvises a shorter distance in curve – or not even in curve, but in kink? Kink is neither curve nor circle, much less line. Indeed, a kink is often said to be a block. And what is a collection of kinks, or a collective of kinks, if not a dread, or jam? Watch me? No, watch meh, motherfucker.

Locating by finding the current longitude and latitude is to miss the opportunity – and all that could happen but cannot be anticipated when one tries – to find something in the midst/amongst everything else along with/in/out which it exists. This manner of locating both specifies and generalizes and, as such, it follows the basic map of what exist Kant's provide in his *Critique of Judgment*, under his law of specification of nature. The image is that of distinguishable wholes within which other smaller wholes lie, each (but for the most general, which he calls Nature) both a part of and a participant of the larger one within which it is found.

In the abstract, this pinpointing of the where of something takes everything else along with it exists out of consideration. Once that is done, shifting something from one where (location) to another (location) can be considered, that is, it is possible to return attention to the whole, the full context within which that thing exists. But then, at that point, as Stefano and Fred recall, it is not even about the thing anymore, it is about movement, the moving of the thing, and the how to do so. Logistics, they note, is about the where and how and to what end of the movement, about the flow and its improvement, about the procedures that will ensure it. That, however, is only possible to think about/with because when attending to what happens, instead of focusing on the what and the how that happens, we presume that it will not unhappen and move on to focus on what made it happen (efficient cause) or on how it was before and after that which made it happen played out.

However, as we know the algorithm that effectuates, the line of commands designed for improving the flow – to address and prevent corruption, deviation, and undesirable re/de/generation – does not, cannot account for itself. As such, it becomes open, exposed to the general un-comprehensible incompleteness in the midst of which it finds itself. Not completely distinguishable from everything found in its most general where – at the smallest and the larger delimited whole – diffusively differing in its many implications, the flow wanes and wanders: it may be even possible that what comes to happen takes place before what has brought it about in the first place. It is indeed that messed up.

Logisticality, our wandering wonders do threaten logistics. Not because it strays, ignoring, stepping over and dancing above the (fault) lines. No! as Harney and Moten remind us: "Kink is neither curve nor circle, much less line" 'cause "a collection of kinks, or a collective of kinks, if not a dread, or jam." Unbounded impropriety of things is that which re/de/generates the social into black sociality, which is the militant practice of *diffunity* that is, the giving incompleteness.

IV.

The undercommons is not, except incidentally, about the university; and the undercommons is crucially about a sociality not based on the individual. Nor, again, would we describe it as derivative of the individual – the undercommons is not about the dividual, or the pre-individual, or the supra-individual. The undercommons is an attachment, a sharedness, a diffunity, a partedness.

Reading *All Incomplete*, over the past few months, as I followed the rising rate of infections and the growing numbers of persons being killed by COVID-19, the disease caused by Sars-CoV-2 (the new corona virus), I could not but wonder about how improvement is at work, in Brazil and in the USA, for instance. Improvement, we know, governs the decisions (by policy makers and algorithms) to let die that are made in view of numbers that show who (the economically dispossessed, "essential workers," with "underlying conditions," who happen to be, in the US, a large percentage of the country's black, Indigenous, Latinx populations). It is the operating element behind what seems to be an accumulation of decisions that led to an increase in the number of infections and deaths. I cannot but wonder about how is that line of reasoning expressed, which words are used which words are avoided. Under other names, invention, progress, civilization, development, improvement is also at work in the previous decisions leading to their economic dispossession, to their underlying conditions, to their finding employment in the economic sectors most exposed during a global pandemic.

Under this global pandemic, it becomes once more evident how improvement guides management of scarcity, in the economy and the polity. Given that which is corrupt or improper is expected to fail to thrive, the logical decision is to protect or preserve what can survive and thrive. Whatever this is, it is capable of improvement – on its own or through policy. What else accounts for the up-to-now unthinkable decision made by health care professionals which was to leave the elderly and underlying-conditions COVID-19 patients off the ventilators, in order to have these available to the 'younger' and 'healthier,' that is, the one who would improve with this treatment. Wasn't it the same logic that, in the global economic crisis of 2007-2008, governments used to justify rescuing major corporations and banks, because they were 'too big to fail'? Though, in this latter case, they had already failed but they were (their share of the world economy is) too big to be let die. What does this mean to the rest of us? The ones too small to thrive? Too frail to live? Who do not count, who in the decision and in the algorithm (in the structure-procedure, algorithm that supports it, that gives it both an end and evidence) figure as null, nothing, no-thing, no-bodies? What about them? How can they possibly exist and persist, knowing that their number is never called because it makes no sense, because it does not fit in the calculation, because it is out of sorts, and up-side-down? Them, who?

since ain't 'nobody looking for us.' So, we look for us with Husni-Bey, and wonder how we turned from, and will turn back to, the infinite rehearsal that turns study mad, or black, in standing with those who have no standing until we've fallen in with them. With us. The complicit. The damned. Then, who determines?

Existence as un-prehensible, undercommons sociality, *All Incomplete* offers us, is not about becoming or coming along. Without plot or plan, as/in flesh or the body approached as/in incessant de/re/composition, which is nothing more than earthly existence. That is not the force of law, of the line that connects, divides, and directs. Jus generativity, which can be read as the quality and capacity to give – not in the context of an economy (as in the managing of scarcity) but as generosity (as in the abundance of the rain forest). That generosity I find in their militant practice of writing-with each other (as well as with all the) others they think-with. That is generosity to me, which is also the way of black sociality, in its impurity and complicity – thank you Fred and Stefano!

THE THEFT OF ASSEMBLY

> If I were asked to answer the following question: *What is slavery?* and I should answer in one word, *It is murder*, my meaning would be understood at once. No extended argument would be required to show that the power to remove a man's mind, will, and personality, is the power of life and death, and that it makes a man a slave. It is murder. Why, then, to this other question: *What is property?* may I not likewise answer, *It is robbery!*, without the certainty of being misunderstood; the second proposition being no other than a transformation of the first?
> – Pierre-Joseph Proudhon

1.
The first theft shows up as rightful ownership. This is the theft of fleshly, earth(l)y life, which is then incarcerated in the body. But the body, it turns out, is just the first principal-agent problem. The body is just an overseer, a factor, a superintendent for the real landlord, the real owner, the individual, in his noxious, heavy-handed conceptuality. The legal term for this principal-agent problem is mind. In this regard, the designation 'mind/body problem' is a synecdochal redundancy in abstraction rather than an entanglement, or even an opposition, of *anima* and matter, mama and soul.

There's this formulation that Robert Duncan gets from Erwin Schrödinger that helps a certain disordering along. Schrödinger says "living matter evades the decay to equilibrium." Well, if Proudhon is right, and slavery, murder, robbery, and property are a unit; if the general regime of private property is most accurately understood as social death; then what if death/private property is that equilibrium of which Schrödinger speaks? What John Donne speaks of by way of God's sovereign capacity to preserve is a problem that will have been meant to solve a problem; and when Schrödinger speaks of evading the decay to equilibrium, he isn't saying that all decay is bad. Corruption is our (accursed) share, our antological practice, our eccentric centering, as M.C. Richards might say. How we evade ownership/equilibrium is given precisely in that refusal to prevent loss that we call sharing, rubbing, empathy, hapticality: the undercommon love of flesh, our essential omnicentric or anacentric eccentricity.

Every thing, in the wake of such disordering, is loss prevention. John Locke creates the tabula rasa as a container for properties – properties of the mind, and properties owned by the propertied mind. Self-knowledge is self-possession and self-positioning in Locke. His accumulation process is auto-location, because one can't help but settle for that. From the first moment, which appears to keep happening all the time, all property is posited, beginning with the positing/positioning of a body for locating ownership, and the owned, and a mind for owning. The posit and the deposit inaugurate ownership as incorporation, whose inevitable end, given in continual withdrawal, is loss. This requires the production of a science of loss, which is to say the science of whiteness, or, logistics.

Every acquisition, every improvement, is an ossification of sharing. This ossification is given in and as containment. The first odious vessel produced by and for logistics is not the slave ship, but the body – flesh conceptualized – which bears the individual-in-subjection. A profound viciousness begins with this colonization of the posited body, the appointment of the posited mind, and the manipulation – in various modalities of brutality – of their mutually enveloping redundancy, given in the dead perpetual motion of the will to colonize. This enclosure, this settlement, will be repeated because it must be repeated. Every slave will have been every time the mirror in which the self, in seeing itself, comes into existence in and as itself, which is an omnicidal fantasy.

Locke invents the derivative here, a degraded part of the accursed share that is poised to draw on the power of this share, but only to create more derivatives, to create more zones of dispossession by positing possession, in the denial of loss that prepares for loss. All property is loss because all property is the loss of sharing. In its willfulness, property is theft; but beyond the murderousness that would attend theft-in-acquisition one mind/body at a time, the theft in question here is absolute serial murder, which we survive only insofar as all property remains vulnerable to sharing. This is to say nothing other than that all property is fugitive. It flees from its own positing, runs from being-deposited. All (property) jumps bail. Sharing, exhaustion, expending, derivation will have been contained and congealed in the measurable and accountable individual unit of the derivative. But sharing is our means, the earth's means in us and our means in earth. Logistics would seem to value means over ends – everything is how to get it there, not what it is – but logistics is really the degradation of means, the general devaluation of means through individuation and privatization, which are the same thing. It is the science of lost means advanced with every act of loss prevention.

If Locke invents the derivative, then Immanuel Kant's innovation is high frequency trading. And when Kant reverses the fortunes of logistics by announcing that it is the ends (of man) and not the means that are important, the human, the ultimate derivative, is fully logistically installed. The human is held up, not by Kant, but by logistics, a logistics that gives the illusion of a free-standing subject. A human universe appears to Kant, full of what he posits as human properties. Kant walks the docks, traversing the seven bridges of Königsberg, surveying the logistical world from a point of view he never needs to leave. From there, his ship come in with each new travel log and ethnographic treatise, he is witness to the humanization of the flesh. Logistics now has a subject and it is race. The humanization of the flesh is the racialization of the flesh. It is the catastrophe that befalls the species-being, one not even Marx can reverse. This is why logistics is the science of whiteness in/as the science of loss.

Such is the peril to flesh/earth by the time of Georg Wilhelm Friedrich Hegel, as Denise Ferreira da Silva teaches. Surveillance. Access. Transparency. Resilience. The globalized, generalized fear of loss is everywhere logistics sees the need to straighten out our tangled flesh. And everywhere logistics finds monstrosity, it humanizes it. Now, to be obscure, as Saidiya Hartman instructs, is to be entangled; it is to be hunted, to be subject to the subject of the grasp. Sub-subjected thus, how can you say that we are persons? Flesh/Earth is assaulted by global improvement, worldly usufruct. With improvement, Hegel produces the regulatory framework called deregulation. Nothing will get in the way of the development of the race, or in the way of the race of developers. Arrayed before and through this is our opacity, given in and as our *otium*, that ante-programmatic disorder R. A. Judy speaks of as our speech, arrayed, as Fumi Okiji does and says, with mouths agape, in the curse, the damnation, the incompleteness that we share.

2.

In Zen Buddhist philosophy the goal of the Heart Doctrine is *ji ji muge*, which can be translated as *no block*. Nothing prevents the path, the way, from flowing. The heart travels freely. But when the heart travels freely it must not imagine it is free. That is why we must also translate *ji ji muge* as *non non block*. The difference between no block and non non block is both infinitely small and infinite. But where to look for this distinction? We have sought this distinction in the difference between diversity and the general antagonism or between touch and hapticality or indeed perhaps most explicitly between logistics and logisticality.

Because what are we to make of the fact that today it is the science of logistics that most *seems* to have realized the Heart Doctrine of Zen Buddhism? It is the science of logistics that dreams of flow without blockage, and tries to turn these dreams into reality. Hard logistics and soft logistics work together. The yang of the Belt and Road and the yin of the algorithm fantasize together of *no block*.

If this is true, we should be worried. In its origins, and its contemporary mutations, logistics is a regulatory force standing against us, standing against the earth. Logistics begins in loss and emptiness. And it begins in a fundamental misapprehension called spacetime. The loss that marks ownership, specifically the ownership of private property, the loss of sharing, the loss of the earth and the consequent making of the world, is simultaneously the misapprehension that what is privatized is empty and will be filled by ownership itself, by properties, by properties placed into it. This emptiness will be filled with an interior. This emptiness is confirmed by logistics, by the mobilization, the colonizing drive, of this interior – where properties are imported into empty space.

This begins, again, with Locke or, at least, we can begin again through him. His concept of the mind as tabula rasa – often portrayed as an Enlightenment move away from predetermination – is a projection of this emptiness that must be owned and filled. For this emptiness to become private property it must be filled with and located in the coordinates of space and time. Space emerges as the delimitation of what is mine, and time begins with the theft and imposition when it became mine. The individual mind and its coming to maturity out of the tabula rasa mark this first conquest. Enlightenment interiority emerged from this *emplotment* of time and space – to borrow from Hayden White – this separation from what is shared. But interiority is only for the owning mind. Because what allows this mind to take possession of itself is its ability to grasp property, which is something it now posits as beyond itself. It takes what it is taken from for what it needs to create itself, and not just needs but compulsively, interminably, voraciously seeks without end. In other words, the emplotment of time and space in the mind takes place through the emplotment of time and space on earth, in a conversion of emptiness into world, and is simultaneously taken as a fulfilment of mind, its interior appointment in and of what can now be conceptualized as body. Is it a leap to say logic and logistics start here inseparably?

This is why there is no separating Locke the Enlightenment thinker from Locke the writer on race, the author of the notorious colonial constitution of the Carolinas. Ownership was a feedback loop – the more you own the more you own yourself. The more logistics you apply the more logic you acquire; the more logic you deploy the more logistics you require. As Hortense Spillers says, the transatlantic slave trade was the supply chain of Enlightenment. It was never-ending quest and conquest, because ownership is perpetual loss. Gilles Deleuze said that he would rather call power "sad." We might say the same of ownership, where lies the most direct sense of loss of sharing. This feeling of loss translates into a diabolical obsession with loss prevention. Logistics emerges as much as the science of loss prevention as the science of moving property through the emptiness, of making the world as it travels by filling it. This is not making the road as we walk, in the anarchist tradition. This is converting everything in its path into a coordinated time and space for ownership.

Such seizing, such grasping, and such loss prevention is the mode of operation for the wickedness of the Atlantic slave trade, the first massive, diabolic, commercial logistics. Already this feedback loop of ownership experiences amplified loss, the loss of sharing, with each emplotment. But now, in taking up the European heritage of race and slavery that Robinson identifies as emerging in the class struggle in Europe in the centuries directly before Locke and extending into Locke's own time, a double loss is experienced, an intensification of the ownership feedback loop (and what we call the subject reaction). This evil emplotment of Africans is experienced as the potential loss of property that can flee. It is in this double loss of sharing – given in owning and in the imposition of being-owned – that the most deadly, planet-threatening, disease of the species-being emerges: whiteness. And it is for this reason that we can say logistics is the white science.

(This is what many white people – who are the people, as James Baldwin says, who think they are white or that they ought to be – are doing when you see them walk straight past a queue of people and take a seat, or move to the center of a crowded room, or speak more loudly than those around them, or block a sidewalk while discussing 'choices' with their toddler. Making theory out of practice, they are emplotted, as they've been taught to do, establishing the spacetime of possession and self-possession in ownership. Every step they take is a standing of ground, a stomping of the world out of earthly existence and into racial capitalist human being. It grows more pronounced the more it is threatened, consumed by its own feedback loop, and it produces sharper and sharper subject reactions in the face of this threat. This is the old/new fascism: not the anonymity of following the leader, but the subject reaction to leadership, which can just as easily imagine itself to be liberal dissent from, as supposedly opposed to a lock(e)-step repetition of, its call.

In emplotted time and space, the shortest distance between two abstract and dimensionless points – the empty spaces that are conjured to be (ful)filled as world, or worlds, or parts of world – is a straight and dimensionless line. Given imaginary extension, nature's nest of boxes is a supply chain, a partnership of trade, a progress of henchmen in the wake of imaginal sovereignty. The basic building blocks of the science of logistics emerge from this narrow geometry as brutalist geography. The Traveling Salesman Problem is the problem of how to extend this idea – that the shortest distance between two points is a straight line – when there are multiple destinations and stops. Of course, logistics has often found this empty earth contains blocks and denies access. But the science builds itself up to overcome these blocks and achieve this access. Logistics aims to straighten us out, untangle us, and open us to its usufruct, its improving use; such access to us, in its turn, improves the flow line, the straight line. And what logistics takes to be the shortest distance between us requires emplotting us as bodies in space where interiority can be imposed even as the capacity for interiority can be denied, in the constant measure and regulation of flesh and earth.

3.

We learn a lot about how logistics works today from Shoshona Zuboff's *The Age of Surveillance Capitalism*, which seeks to defend interiority against surveillance capitalism's predatory economic logic.[1] Zuboff argues that information technology now makes its money from gathering, packaging and selling massive amounts of data on our everyday behavior. Thus, Facebook or Google do not make money by targeting your tastes or behavior with advertisements as is commonly assumed. According to Zuboff, they have no interest in us individually, though that does not mean these tools do not also individuate. Rather, it is the aggregate data that matters because it can be used not to track but to change behavior. She notes, moreover, that intervening in aggregate provides even more valuable aggregate data. Facebook is spying on you only insofar as it is spying on us, according to Zuboff; and if we are its raw material, and its product, then her employment of the concept of primitive accumulation is justified. Problematically, this argument appears to assume capital without labor, labor having been replaced by an algorithm that will have carried out itself. But what we learn from the Italian autonomists, and from centuries of theorization by Africans experiencing the nightmare of total subsumption, which Zuboff's assumption of absent work extends, is that we are raw material, product, and labor, too. Our work makes this economic logic, or any economic logic, work. And what is the nature of our work in surveillance capitalism? Logistics. We bear, in the obsessive self-management of 'our' clicks and strokes, the overdetermination logistics lays down. It is both through and as a set of applications we apply – both on and underneath a field of platforms we erect – that our labor further concentrates the means of production with the goal quite simply and starkly of preventing us from taking care of one another, from looking out for one another, by making us look at one another, which is taking care of them.

Indeed, the more we look at Zuboff even on her own terms, the more we notice that the other side of modification is *prevention*. To move a part of a population one way is to prevent it from moving another. Soon this logistics of surveillance capitalism seems to be as much about blockage as flow, something that would, of course, be consistent with us being not just raw material, not just product, but socializing labor, as well. In any case, the blockages of surveillance capitalism, of logistical capitalism more generally, raise a question. If their logistics both assumes and dictates that the shortest distance between two points is a straight line, what if our logisticality, before and against both assumption and dictation, improvises a shorter distance in curve – or not even in curve, but in kink? Kink is neither curve nor circle, much less line. Indeed, a kink is often said to be a block. And what is a collection of kinks, or a collective of kinks, if not a dread, or jam? Watch me? No, watch meh, motherfucker.

Which brings us to the story of Leonard Percival Howell.[2] As if enslavement, indenture, and domination were not enough, imperialized people were also named. So, Powell preferred to go by the name Gangunguru Maragh, or Gong, for short, or Tuff Gong, for even shorter. Gong came from a place named Clarendon, Jamaica. Not all of Jamaica is good for growing sugar, but this part is. After emancipation the British retained their wicked sweet tooth and so, as with so many places in the empire, they redoubled what Édouard Glissant calls "arrowlike nomadism" of the Conquistadors in Clarendon with displaced people from the Indian subcontinent, who were settled, unsettled, and resettled in, while also being indentured to, coloniality's cold logistics and brutal algorithms.[3] Gong, who had worked with Marcus Garvey's organization, and travelled the world, was looking for an anti-colonial faith, after fighting regularly with the English Church in Jamaica. He knew that church – the Church of Logistics, the 'Christianity' of surveillance, the true religion of colonial rule – could never bear the faith he sought, the faith he found(ed) when he (re)turned to the insurgent homelessness of his home. It was in the indentured, Hindu workers from India that he saw proof that each people had to find their true religion. He spent time with them in Clarendon, observing their tea ceremonies with ganja and their Ital diets. He named himself from their language – Gan or Gyan for wisdom; Gun for faith; Guru for teacher; and Maragh for king. Soon Gangunguru Maragh set about building the true religion, as he saw it, of the black man.

He never wore dreadlocks but with his dreadlocked followers he made a village in Sligoville, called Pinnacle, which British authorities described as socialist. They tried repeatedly to destroy it, and they confined Gong in their newly opened mental asylum. But Rastafarianism would be neither destroyed nor confined, which is something to consider if you are sitting in 'Slave Island' in old Colombo, Sri Lanka. The Portuguese brought Africans here in the sixteenth century, but the coasts of Colombo and those of East Africa have always looked across at each other. As Vijay Prashad and May Joseph teach us, African maharajahs have sat on thrones in India and the commerce and cultural exchange between Sri Lanka and East Africa is ancient.[4] And yet it was not this straight distance between two points, this straight journey from South Asia to East Africa, that Gong travelled, or that his indentured companions in the villages of Clarendon travelled, to be with each other. The knot, the tangle, the embrace; the puff, the jam, the kink they came upon and carried is the shorter distance, where watch meh means watch with me for one hour, while we gather all together one more time.

The Zen heart travels without block. But we might also say it travels with nothing blocking it. And as we know first from Taoist philosophy, nothingness is not emptiness. It is not space. When the Zen heart travels through nothing, nothing is its constant companion. Nothing is the block through which it travels, on which it stands, in which it hangs. The block that makes no block into non non block. Nothing, naught, knot gives the Zen heart its directionless directions, its wandering syncopations, its tight-knit-open pansyncretic practices, allowing, in compelling, us to visit and renew. The unwatchable place we make when we watch with one another, having refused to watch one another, having refused one and another, is shared, unblocked, unloaded into a kink, the non non block of our stranded strand.

Watch meh, shorter distance, ji ji muge!

WE WANT A PRECEDENT

1.
Our President, our deluded and degraded and demonic sovereign, in whatever form this abstraction of our abstract and wholly fictional equivalence will have taken, is a featureless point on a long and hopelessly straight line of knock-offs. It's like how Richard of Bordeaux, who can do whatever he wants except stop himself from doing whatever he wants, carries around his own deposition (disguised as the serial murder that constitutes the peaceful transition of power and its vulgar ceremonies) like a genetic flaw, as the illegitimate but inevitably heritable Bolingbroke-ass ambitions that leave him with ever increasingly etiolated capacities for self-reflection. So that in all its singularly focused limitation and qualification, in the relative nothingness of the prison that it calls a world, the all-encompassing and all to be settled sphere that it stomps all over all the time, posing for an impossible arc of deadly and impossible pictures, our President, whichever one you ever wanted or didn't want, each one after the other in noticeable imperial decline, is just a sick, uneasy head in a hollow crown, making us watch it talk about how it's gonna kill us and then making us watch it kill us.

2.
What we want is usually said to be all bound up with what we don't have. Zoe Leonard's been talking about what we want, though, slantedly, in the

dimensionless infinity room we can't even crawl around in when we cruise the rub and whirr of the city as a grove of aspen in late fall, in the mountains, held and unheld at the bottom of the sea. She's talking about what we want in relation to what we have when what we have is all this experience of not having, of shared nothing, of sharing nothingness. She speaks of and from a common underprivilege, from the privilege of the common underground, in and from the wealth of a precarity that goes from hand to hand, as a caress. Look at all the richness we have, she says, in having lost, in having suffered, in having been suffered, in suffering one another as if we were one another's little children, as if we were in love with one another, as if we loved one another so much that all one and another can do is go. We want a president, Zoe says, who's loved and lost all that with us, who's shared our little all, our little nothing. Such a thing, the general and generative nothingness that is more and less than political, would be unprecedented. Maybe she doesn't want a president; maybe she wants a precedent, the endlessly new thing of the absolutely no thing, its Zen xenogenerosity, its queer reproductivity, which keeps on beginning in beginning's absence as ungoverned and ungovernable care(ss).

3.

Is it possible to want what you have become in suffering, both in the absence and in the depths of suffrage, without wanting what it is to suffer? Can you want what it is to be all, and want what it is to be whole, without wanting to be complete? Is it possible to crave the general incompleteness without that seemingly unbearable desire to be pierced, ruptured, broken? In lieu of the president we want and don't want, we have Cedric Robinson, whom just a little while ago we lost. He says:

> If, in some spiteful play, one were compelled by some demon or god to choose a transgression against Nietzsche so profound and fundamental to his temperament and intention as to break apart the ground on which his philosophy stood, one could do no better than this: a society which has woven into its matrix for the purpose of suspending and neutralizing those forces antithetic to individual autonomy, the constructed reality that *all are equally incomplete. A logic is being jousted here.* Is it not so that the emergence of power as the instrument of certainty in human organization is seen by many to be the *consequence of* and response to the circumstances of inequality and sensed social entropy? Is it not so that individual autonomy, rare enough in the first condition and imperiled by the second, is in the final construction made foreign? And does not, logically, even

autonomy require for its nurturance a hothouse of certitude similar to that required for the evolution of power – autonomy being to a degree a variant of power?

Then the principle of incompleteness – the absence of discrete organismic integrity, if it were to occupy in a metaphysics the place of inequality in political philosophy, would bring to human society a paradigm subversive to political authority as the archetypical resolution, as the prescription for order.[5]

How can we come more accurately to understand American democracy – the brutality of our improvement, the viciousness of the ways we are put to use – as the praxis of privatized interest in inequality, expressed in the theory of the abstract equality of every complete individual, whose constant recitation brutally regulates the general interest in an equality given in and as an absolute incompleteness that defies individuation? How can we come to understand that the interinanimation of our bondage and our freedom – and, therefore, of our liberalism and our protest – is the metaphysical foundation of a national political philosophy that *we have come to claim in violation of the precedent we want.* How can we disavow that claim, having learned to want to want the order from which our forced desire is derived to be drowned in the disorder

of all (the nothing) we have? How can we more intensely feel the physics of our surround, our social aesthetic, the gravity of our love and loss, our shared, radically sounded, radically sent incompleteness? What would it mean to say we cannot take a position on politics – even the old and honorable 'I don't vote because I'm Marxist' position? What if we said we have no options, that here we don't even have the option of no option? We think that would be good. Zoe gets us started: to think *off* of what we want is lightly to inhabit not being and not having, *here*.

USUFRUCT AND USE

1.

THE IDEA THAT MODERNITY IS, PROPERLY SPEAKING, THE GLOBALIZATION OF Europe" is what Tsenay Serequeberhan calls the pre-text of the European Enlightenment, that "metaphysical belief or idea (*Idee*) that European existence is qualitatively superior to other forms of human life."[6] This metaphysical belief is grounded in the very idea of Europe as geographical and geopolitical embodiment and exception. The European exception has certainly been well diagnosed. Critics of colonialism and its rampant episteme, most notably Sylvia Wynter, have noted that one cannot produce the self-owning, earth-owning individual without producing the figure of man, whose essential inhumanity is evident in his restless theorizing and practicing of race. For how could a self-owning, earth-owning man *not* belong to a self-owning group instantiated in and on a self-owning world that is, at once, an absolute and expansive locale? The self-owning, earth-owning group sets itself apart from other groups – particularly, fundamentally, in violent speciation, from groups that do not own (either self or earth). The cost of this speciation, which is carried out in invasion and enclosure, accrues to those with whom the ones who would be one say they don't belong, as a matter of blood and soil – those whose failure to (want to) be exceptional constitutes a sub- or pre-European (southern or eastern or negro or immigrant or terrorist) problem/question. What is implied in imagining that one has become (exceptional)? There will have been the gift to Europe of its own place, at once insular and unlimited, and its own singular and subdivisible time. This transcendental honorarium, wherein gift is conceptualized as the given and the given is conceptualized as gift, will have granted Europe (the) world as the place and time of exception. But someone will have had to except Europe, to allow the constantly emergent state of its exception, to sacralize its politico-theological ground and atmosphere. Someone will have had to give to Europe(ans) the capacity to be one. (Some)one will have given man the power of being one, a completeness that will have been as if it were given. It is by way, and not in spite, of all this that we speak, in echo of Frantz Fanon, of "that same Europe where they are never done talking of Man" as "an avalanche of murders," a bloody history of slavery and colonialism that suggests the exception is always insufficiently granted and involuntarily accepted, that it is the illusory object of an empty will's incapacity for self-imposition. If the assertion of the European exception is its condition of im/possibility, then the avalanche of murders is that assertion's expressive operation.

Exception is a categorization one grants oneself only at the price of imagining that it has been granted by an Other. To declare one's exceptionalism is not a matter of exempting, or excluding, or excusing oneself, all of which are transitive. Exceptionalism imagines the intransitive and attributes action to Others and, more importantly, an originary kind of power to someone else. And it is here that we see how the pre-text Serequeberhan identifies is in fact pre-given in a double sense – it must be given but in order to be given it must also have been granted. There is no dialectic here. Rather, we might say it is only the European who has ever been both master and slave. This is his drama. It is held in the body, and enacted in the world, that he has to have. The exception will have been a power given by an Other to selves who, in taking it and its accompanying knowledge on, are supposed to have been provided, in this give and take, their own confirmation. But the pre-text is never truly grounded, never truly granted, never truly given. Europe is constantly disestablished by what it seeks to envelop, which, in and out of turn, envelops it. What surrounds the European even in his midst is the native informant Gayatri Spivak identifies as a creation text for a world of exception, against, but nonetheless within, the general antagonism of earthly anarrhythmia and displacement. The paradox of the pre-text is thus that being exceptional can no more be taken than it can be given and can no more be claimed than it can be granted. This simultaneity of being-master and being-slave is sovereignty's static, omnicidal decline. This is what it is to be chained to the struggle for freedom, a 'rational' instrument run amok in place, as man's perpetually stilled motion.

2.

What does it mean to stand for improvement? Or worse, to stand for what business calls a 'commitment to continuous improvement'? It means to stand for the brutal speciation of all. To take a stand for speciation is the beginning of a diabolical usufruct. Improvement comes to us by way of an innovation in land tenure, where individuated ownership, derived from increasing the land's productivity, is given in the perpetual, and thus arrested, becoming of exception's miniature. This is to say that from the outset, the ability to own – and that ability's first derivative, self-possession – is entwined with the ability to make more productive. In order to be improved, to be rendered more productive, land must be violently reduced to its productivity, which is the regulatory diminishment and management of earthly generativity. Speciation is this general reduction of the earth to productivity and submission of the earth to techniques of domination that isolate and enforce particular increases in and accelerations of productivity. In this regard, (necessarily European) man, in and as the exception, imposes speciation upon himself, in an operation that extracts and excepts himself from the earth in order to confirm his supposed dominion over it. And just as the earth must be forcefully speciated to be possessed, man must forcefully speciate himself in order to enact this kind of possession. This is to say that racialization is present in the very idea of dominion over the earth; in the very idea and enactment of the exception; in the very nuts and bolts of possession-by-improvement. Forms of racialization that both Michel Foucault and, especially and most vividly, Robinson identify in medieval Europe become *usufructed* with modern possession through improvement. Speciated humans are endlessly improved through the endless work they do on their endless way to becoming Man. This is the usufruct of man. In early modern England, establishing title to land by making it more productive meant eliminating biodiversity and isolating and breeding a species – barley or rye or pigs. Localized ecosystems were aggressively transformed so that monocultural productivity smothers anacultural generativity. The emergent relation between speciation and racialization is the very conception and conceptualization of the settler. Maintenance of that relation is his vigil and his eve. For the encloser, possession is established through improvement – this is true for the possession of land and for the possession of self. The Enlightenment is the universalization/globalization of the imperative to possess and its corollary, the imperative to improve. However, this productivity must always confront its contradictory impoverishment: the destruction of its biosphere and its estrangement in, if not from, entanglement, both of which combine to ensure the liquidation of the human differential that is already present in the very idea of man, the exception. To stand for such improvement is to invoke policy, which attributes depletion to the difference, which is to say the wealth, whose simultaneous destruction and accumulation policy is meant to operationalize. This attribution of a supposedly essential lack, an inevitable and supposedly natural diminution, is achieved alongside the imposition of possession-by-improvement. To make policy is to impose speciation upon everybody and everything, to inflict impoverishment in the name of improvement, to invoke the universal law of the usufruct of man. In this context, continuous improvement, as it emerged with decolonization and particularly with the defeat of national capitalism in the 1970s, is the continuous crisis of speciation in the surround of the general antagonism. This is the contradiction Robinson constantly invoked and analyzed with the kind of profound and solemn optimism that comes from being with, and being of service to, your friends.

3.

At the end of the movie *Devil in a Blue Dress*, which is based on the Walter Mosley novel of the same name, and which Robinson delighted in teaching us how to read and see, what comes sharply into relief is the persistent life – which survives under the rule of speciation; which surrounds the speciation that would envelop it; which violates the speciation by which it is infused; which anticipates the speciation that would be its end – of a neighborhood of neat lawns, small family houses, and the Black people who live in them. The movie's last line simultaneously belies and acknowledges speciation's permanent crisis. "Is it wrong to be friends with someone you know has done bad things?" asks the movie's protagonist, Easy Rawlins. All you got is your friends, replies Deacon Odell. That's right. That's all. Tomorrow the cops could come back, or the bank, bringing the violence of speciation, against which there is just this constant and general economy of friendship – not the improvement that will have been given in one-to-one relation but the militant preservation of what you (understood as we) got, in common dispossession, which is the only possible form of possession, of having in excess of anyone who has. Neither the globalization of possession-by-improvement nor the achievement of being exceptional is possible. We live (in) the brutality of their failure, which is a failure in and as derivation. Moreover, the sovereign declension (given, in a variation of Silva's grammar as God: Patriarch – Possessive Individual – Citizen) is a derivative – a rigid, reified, securitized understanding of difference. Meanwhile, in the scene it constantly sets on Easy's porch, in Joppy's bar, at John's Place (the illegal club above Hattie Mae's grocery store), *Devil in a Blue Dress* keeps reminding us that the task at hand is, as Manolo Callahan would say, to renew our habits of assembly, which implies a turn, a step away from the derivative. We ain't studying the failure, just like Easy ain't studying no job. We ain't trying to enter the declension that instigates what it implies: the (necessarily failed) separation, speciation, and racialization – the enclosure and settlement – of the earth. The play, as Callahan and Nahum Chandler teach us, is to desediment, to exfoliate, to renew the earthly and inseparable assembly, the habitual jam, by way of and in the differentiation of what will be neither regulated nor understood. All we got is us in this continual giving away of all. And, as Robinson also took great care to teach us in his critical admiration of Easy's friend Mouse, who is always about to blow somebody's nose off, all depends upon our readiness to defend it.

4.

Here is the famous passage on slavery in *Elements of the Philosophy of Right* where the "not yet" – its phase as mere "natural human existence" – of the universal appears as a tainted and unnecessary remedy:

> If we hold firmly to the view that the human being in and for himself is free, we thereby condemn slavery. But if someone is a slave, his own will is responsible, just as the responsibility lies with the will of a people if that people is subjugated… Slavery occurs in the transitional phase between natural human existence and the truly ethical condition; it occurs in a world where a wrong is still right. Here, the wrong *is valid*, so that the position it occupies is a necessary one.[7]

This "not yet" of the universal, of global history, is subsequently reinforced when Hegel says, "The same determination [absolute right] entitles civilized nations to regard and treat as barbarians other nations which are less advanced than they are in the substantial moments of the state."[8] But before then, Hegel immediately turns from the first passage and towards the subject of "taking possession" and the "use of the thing." This "natural entity" – the thing – exists only for its owner, for "since this realized externality is the use or employment to which I subject it, it follows that *the whole use* or employment of it is *the thing in its entirety*."[9] But then Hegel reaches a problem, just after paradoxically asserting the necessary rectitude of the necessary wrong of slavery in progressive history.

> If the whole extent of the use of a thing were mine, but the abstract ownership were supposed to be someone else's, the thing as mine would be wholly penetrated by my will… while it would at the same time contain something impenetrable by me, i.e. the will, in fact the empty will, of someone else.[10]

He calls this a relationship of "absolute contradiction" and then introduces the Roman idea of "*usufructus.*"[11] In theory, Hegel is addressing feudal property rights, with their shared ownership. But it is he in "natural human existence" who has failed, as Hegel says in his previous consideration of slavery, to take "possession of himself and become his own property." Usufruct demands this natural entity be "subordinated to its useful aspect." Hegel speaks of Roman and feudal property, but his concern is world history, this (necessarily European) world where a wrong is still right. His concern is with how to become one's own property and with the usufruct that initiates and confounds this project. Improvement is granted and haunted by an illusory and impenetrably empty will.

5.

The moment you say it is mine because I worked on it and improved it, or you say that I am me because I worked on myself and improved myself, you start a war. And by misattributing the initiation of this war to nature, you then codify this war as the (anti)social contract.

It is said that the (anti)social contract and the public sphere it creates is a reaction to feudalism and absolutism. But this is only half the story, and an inaccurate half at that. Perhaps it's better to think of the (anti)social contract as emerging, as Angela Mitropoulos says, not in opposition to absolutism but as the democratization of sovereignty. Even that might have had an inadvertently anarchic quality, as every man considered himself a king. But the (anti)social contract not only reacts to, while also reflecting, absolutism, making every home/castle/hovel a hall of mirrors, it also emerges as a way to explain and justify the violence of European man. Everyone from Adam Ferguson to Immanuel Kant tries to explain why the Africans, Asians, and indigenous people being exterminated and enslaved are so much less warlike than Europeans. The Crusades misled Europeans into believing their brutality was part of humanity rather than an exception, even as religious war gave them a taste for blood that they could not ignore. So the (anti)social contract emerges less to confront absolutism than to contain the obvious historical exceptionalism of European savagery. Clearly the world could not be ordered around good and evil without some dire consequences for Europe. Those who conceive of the (anti)social contract mistake the wars it instigates: wars of sovereigns against contractors, and of contractors against each other, and of contractors against those whom Bryan Wagner describes as "being subject to exchange without being a party to exchange," the ones who are not one who are innumerable and un(ac)countable even in having been accumulated, even in having been financialized.[12] Perhaps, in this regard, it would be even better to think of the (anti)social contract as emerging against a history of revolt: the peasant revolts that buried European feudalism, and which Robinson understands as "the socialist exchange" comprising Marxism's anthropological (under)ground, is the revolt of nature, prosecuted by those who are made to stand in for nature, having been philosophically relegated to some essentially paradoxical state of nature by the ones who seek to engineer nature's subordination to and within the socioecological disaster of improvement.

This is to say, again, that the political half of the story, in which the social contract is understood as improvement rather than its ge(n)ocidal imposition, is wrong and incomplete. The (anti)social contract is not only a political theory but also an economic practice: the practice of the juridical regulation and antisocialization of exchange in the imposition of improvement. In particular, the social contract specified the individuation of its parties. Individuals now must be formed in order to enter into contract. And the economic contract emerges not in exchange but from the idea that ownership derives from improvement. As a result, it is not simply the individual, but rather the individual capable of self-improvement, who must and can enter into the contract. The self-improving individual can also be thought of as the self-accumulating individual: not possessive (this is stasis without movement), not acquiring (this still bears the trace of anarchic exchange), but self-accumulating – that is, property-gathering in order to put property to work, including and most especially the properties of the self that can be deployed and improved while being posited as eternal and absolute. "Properties of the self" is not a pun here. Properties that can be accumulated and put to work include race, religion, and gender but also class, standing, trust, thrift, reliability, and punctuality. These can all be used to improve where to improve is to own, and own more, and thus set in motion further accumulation of self, others, and nature that all might be put to work.

Maybe it can be stated this way: ownership emerges in Europe as usufruct, in the improvement of land that grants and justifies it. It is extended and diffused throughout the regime the social contract defines in the self-ownership that will have taken its completed form in the individual – that brutal, brittle crystallization of an always and necessarily incomplete melding of subject and object. Ceaselessly at work in the task of making everything, including himself, subject to being put to work, the European is the usufruct of man. Man's endless improvement, in which necessity is enforced as an absolute contingency, is fixed in European thought as the vicious grasping of its objects, including itself. The historical unfolding of this fixation on fixing, the murderous interplay of capture and improvement, is given in and as *self*-improvement-in-*self*-accumulation's violence towards whatever shows up at the rendezvous of differentiation, incompletion, and affection. The constantly changing activity of what appears to what appears as the self as the continual undoing of the very idea of the self and its eternally prospective completion-in-improvement can only be met, from the self's myopic and impossible perspective, with a nasty combination of regulation and accumulation. The one who accumulates does so at the expense of what it takes to be its others – women, slaves, peasants, beasts, the earth itself. Thus, the social contract, as a contract between the improving and accumulating ones, is inscribed upon the flesh of those who cannot be, and in any case refuse to be, a party to antisocial exchange under the terms of the (anti)social contract. Meanwhile, as much as the contractors are united in a strategy to subject to usufruction whatever cannot or will not be a (numerable, individuated) party to antisocial exchange, they are also dedicated to killing each other, to war in and as their beloved public carried out in the name of the improvement of that public and its problems – that is, its denizens. The self-accumulating individual's war, his total mobilization against the innumerable and against his fellows under the sign of ownership as improvement, carried out in order to prevent the recrudescence of the natural, renders irredeemable the very premise of the (anti)social contract.

And every subcontract within the (anti)social contract must result in improvement. It's not a matter of both parties being satisfied with what they have exchanged. Such a contract was not just badly made but at odds with the desired identity of the contractors. And here we can put it the other way around: the social contract is conceived by the political theorists also as a contract amongst those capable of self-improvement, or what they called progress, and this is why it was essentially destructive of the notions of exchange encountered amongst feudal rebels (Robinson's *An Anthropology of Marxism* is instructive here) or of exchange encountered amongst Africans who would rather move elsewhere than enter into conflict to gain improvement (Robinson's *Black Marxism* is instructive here).[13] Ferguson and Kant both say war is about improvement of the European race. And Robinson teaches us that this is carried out as a violent intra-European racialization of difference, a continually barbaric festival in which incursion and the instantiation of improvement as militarily enforced externalities produce Europe, and then the globe, as dead and deadly bodies politic, monsters whose mechanized, drone-like simulations of spirit regulate the social with the kind of latex affability and latent menace commonly associated with police commissioners and university provosts. Antisocial sociability is the basis of the social contract. In the end, improvement is war, which is why the public sphere is war, and why the private – in its anti- and ante-individual impurity, as refuge even under constant pressure – is a porch.

The (anti)social contract is haunted by the economic contract, which is not a contract of exchange like one might find in friendship, but a contract based on the claim to ownership of oneself, others, and nature that is always tied to what more one can make of, which is to say accumulate in and through, oneself, others, and nature. In other words, the expanding universe of ownership took a contractual form that was not limited, as is sometimes supposed, to free individuals – that is, to the European subject imagined by the European theorist; it is a contractual form, rather, that requires broad-spectrum contact as the material ground of its exclusive and exclusionary network. What makes it truly dangerous is that it could never get free of that from which it wished to distinguish itself; what is truly dangerous to it is that what is forced to grant its exception can refuse the contract to which it is a third (or an innumerable or a non-)party. Exchange, on the other hand, is a practice that prevents accumulation at, and as the elimination of, its source – the self-improving individual. Instead, exchange, given in and as the differential and differentiating entanglement of social life, even under the most powerful forms of constraint and regulation, is about a social optimum.

6.

George Clinton teaches us this:

> I'm always waiting to see what dance they're gonna do, because dance is always changing. But I trust the fact that funk affects the booty. So when I see somebody doing some type of dance, I always try to figure out what groove does it take to make the booty move like that? I'm really a bootyologist. I don't just look at it cause it looks good, but how can I make sure with my music, the booty is at its optimum?[14]

And Jacques Derrida teaches us to ask:

> When will we be ready for an experience of freedom and equality that is capable of respectfully experiencing that friendship, which would at last be just, just beyond the law, and measured up against its measurelessness?[15]

It's just that we could only learn these lessons from them in having learned first from Robinson that the social optimum derives from social wealth, stepping out only to step back in all good, optimally, even under absolute duress, as the preservation in friendship of the socio-ontological totality. Like him, we look forward to getting back to the optimum we never left.

LEAVE OUR MIKES ALONE

> Daughter of Zion, Judah the Lion
> He redeemeth, and bought us with his blood…
> John the revelator, great advocator
> Gets 'em on the battle of Zion
> – Blind Willie Johnson

> When my brother fell
> I picked up his weapons.
> I didn't question
> whether I could aim
> or be as precise as he.
> A needle and thread
> were not among
> his things
> I found.
> – Essex Hemphill

> When we walk down the street
> We don't care who we see or who we meet
> Don't need to run, don't need to hide
> 'cause we got something burning inside
> we've got love   power
> it's the greatest power of them all

> we've got love   power
> and together we can't fall.
> – Luther Vandross

> At times, this land will shake your understanding of the world
> and confusion will eat away at your sense
> of humanity
> but at least you will feel normal.
> – Vernon Ah Kee

The Rebelator

In *Upon Westminster Bridge,* Mikey Smith is jaywalking through the language.[16] It's 1982, the beginning of logistical capitalism. The assembly line is snaking out of the factory and into his mouth. And he cyaan believe it. He won't believe it. He won't go to work. He comes from the property. He's been there before. He's come to undo. He's moved to dissemble. The gathering in his mouth is out of line.

With the rise of logistical capitalism, it is not the product that is never finished but the production line, and not the production line, but its improvement. In logistical capitalism it is the continuous improvement of the production line that never finishes, that's never done, that's undone continuously. The sociologists caught a glimpse of this line and thought that they were seeing networks. The political scientist called this line globalization. The business professors named it and priced it as business process re-engineering. Mikey knew better.

Mikey veers back across the street to where Louise Bennett sits, talking about how she inspired him. We can see her in a clip, wronging rights with her words, advocate of an undone language open to respecting what you like, and liking what you respect. Now her words are everywhere, like whispers from a cotton tree, and they have to be. And logistics, which is to say access, is everywhere – again, because it wants to be.

But not just logistics; and not just any kind of access. The capitalist science of logistics can be represented by a simple formula: movement + access. But logistical capitalism subjects that formula to the algorithm: total movement + total access. Logistical capitalism seeks total access to your language, total translation, total transparency, total value from your words. And then it seeks more. At Queen Mary, University of London, before the counterinsurgency, we called this postcolonial capitalism. How does it feel to be a problem in someone else's supply chain? What else is a colonial regime but the imposition of psychopathic protocols of total access to bodies and land in the service of what today is called supply-chain management? The problem of the twenty-first century is the problem of the color line of assembly.

This logistical capitalism, this postcolonial capitalism, uses the stored, stolen, historical value of words to press its point. But Mikey would not speak that way. He saw what was coming by misremembering what had come to pass. Mikey jay-walked through his audience as they listened the wrong way across his words. Mikey put his hands up to fight one night and surrendered to us. He fought, and by fighting surrendered to, what M. Jacqui Alexander called our "collectivized self-possession," to our hapticality, which is at the same time our collectivized dispossession.[17] Because a rebelator defends our partiality, our incompleteness, our hands dispossessed to hold one another up in the battle of Zion. Mikey was a rebelator in the battle of Zion. Mikey the Rebelator sabotaging a line of words(worth).

Mikey is talking to C. L. R. James on a bed in Brixton in South London, in an unsettled room, Linton Kwesi Johnson standing to the side. You have to move across the language because the language moves the line through you. The line moves now, the assembly line, the flow line, the high line, and that means you. You're moving to work like you always did but now you're working as you're moving, too. James is telling them he used to love Wordsworth and still does, but it was only when he got back to the Caribbean that he realized what was missing in that poetry because something else in that poetry was everywhere. James is talking about language as domination; Mikey is already having to deal with language as forced improvement in production, on the new and improved line, where the Man gives orders to His men. Mikey's working on an old new open secret logisticality, born in the hold, held together in loss and in being lost, and James is giving him some uncoordinates, a sea captain like Ranjit's father, high on the land now, low, shipped, stranded on a bed in Brixton, in an unsettled room. Mikey's not working on improving the English language. He's working on disproving it.

Mikey Smith deregulates the Queen's English in 'Mi Cyaan Believe It' and he's not worried about being incomplete. He's jaywalking through the Queen's English, instituting a sound system to which her standard submits, right across down there so. He's walking across to it right now, on the gully side. Mikey the rebelator. He says that those have "been restless a full time, dem go get some rest." But there's no rest with access; access troubles the unrest it came to steal, and still. This is the early moment of logistical capitalism, with James on the bed aged from industrial capitalism, and all that settler capitalism sedimented underneath them in London in the hard-red earth. In an unsettled room they institute. They're the offline institute of the new line, the new poetics of the anti-line, the antillean, multi-matrilinear dispersion of drum and bass and grain against the grain of organized saying, catching logistics in logisticality's crosstown traffic, in crosstown traffic's constant violation of the crosswalk, the sanctioned intersection, the settled, hegemonic term. Mikey's more and less than perpendicular swerve cyaan believe that managed disturbance and keeps on fucking it up as a field of hypermusical staying, crossed between crossing and forgetting, contradicting and misremembering, revealing and rebelling, refusing to believe. Look the wrong way before you cross. Move the wrong way when you cross. That's how we semble.

When we move we move to access, which is to say we assemble and disassemble anew. And in logistical capitalism the assembly line moves with us by moving through us, accessing us to move and moving us to access. We can't deny access, because access is how we roll, and roll on, in and as our undercommon affectability, as Silva might say.[18] But we make access burn and we love that, the line undone in the undoing of every single product, our renewed assembly in the general disassembly, our dissed assembly offline on the line, strayed staying, stranded beneath the strand, at rest only in unrest, making all the wrong moves, because our doing and undoing ain't the same as theirs. They know, sometimes better than we do, that to move wrong, or not to move, is now no longer just an obstruction to logistics or an obstacle to progress. To move wrong or not to move is sabotage. It is an attack on the assembly line, a subversion of logistical capitalism. To move wrong is to deny access to capital

by staying in the general access that capital desires and devours and denies. To move wrong, to move nought, is to have our own thing of not having, of handing and being handed; it is our continuous breaking up – before, and against that, we were told – of our continuous get together. But with the critical infrastructure that is the new line, and with the resilient response that protects it, the jaywalker becomes no longer just a rube in the way of logistics, a country bukee in traffic, but a saboteur, a terrorist, a demon. Jaywalkers do not sabotage by exodus or occupation as once a maroon, or a striking miner, or a ghost dancer may have. Jaywalkers disturb the production line, the work of the line, the assembly line, the flow line, by demanding inequality of access for all. When the line don't stop to let you catch your breath, jaywalkers stand around and say this stops today. Jaywalking is dissed assembly for itself. Such sabotage is punishable by death. It's hard to know what we institute when we don't institute but we do know what it feels like.

Total value and its violence not only never went away, but as Silva says, they are the foundation of the present as time, the condition of time, of the world as a time-space logic founded on the first horrible logistics of sale, the first mass movement of total access.[19] Now continuous improvement drives us toward total value, makes all work incomplete, makes us move to produce, compels us to get online. We are liberated from work in order to work more, to work harder. We are violently invited to exercise our right to connect, our right to free speech, our right to choose, our right to evaluate, our right to right individuality in order that we may improve the production line running through our liberal dreams. Freedom through work was never the slave's cry but we hear it all around us today. Continuous improvement is the metric and metronomic meter of uplift. Those who won't improve, those who won't collectivize and individuate with the correct neurotic correctness, those who do the same thing again, those who revise, those who tell the joke you've heard and cook the food you've had and take the walk you've walked, those who plan to stay and keep on moving, those who keep on moving wrong – those are the ones who hold everybody back, fucking up the production line that's supposed to improve us all. They like being incomplete. They like being incomplete and incompleting one another. Their incompleteness is said to be a dependency, a bad habit. They're said to be partial, patchy, sketchy. They lack coordinates. They're collectively uncoordinated in total rhythm. They're in(self)sufficient.

Paolo Friere thought our incompleteness is what gave us hope.[20] It is our incompleteness that inclines us toward one another. For Friere, the more we think of ourselves as complete, finished, whole, individual, the more we cannot love or be loved. Is it too much to put this the other way around? To say, by way of Friere, that love is the undercommon self-defense of being-incomplete? This seems important now when our incompleteness is something we are invited and then compelled to address and improve, when we are told to be impatient with it, and embarrassed by it. We need to be intact. We're told to raise our buzz because we're all fucked up. But in our defense, we love that we are complete only in a plained incompletion, which they would have undone, finished, owned, and sent on down the line. We do mind working because we do mind dying.

The Consultant

The consultant is not here to provide solutions, innovation, or even advice. The consultant exists to demonstrate access in the era of logistical capitalism. The consultant is not an ideologue. Ideology operates here only for the consultant himself. He is demonstrably the only one who believes his bullshit, but fortunately for him this is not the point, not his point. The consultant literalizes access to workplaces, demonstrating their openness by showing up in their midst, like a drone. One day you come to work and there he is sitting next to the boss. Nothing she says or does is as important as this demonstration of access. What the consultant introduces into the imposed, exposed workers' corps is the algorithm. The consultant bears the algorithm, which violates in the name of completion. When the consultant brings his algorithmic charge, the body of the workers, that undesired and constantly invaded enclosure, is finished. We are rendered complete, made free, by the work, in the work, of the algorithm. We are done, and done in by, the consultant's forced, aggressive incorporation of an undoing that was of and for itself, of and for ourself, the undoing we keep on making in the face of every sovereign invasion, every violent ascription of words and worth and (the) work. The consultant completes, so that he can access the private loop of a thwarted desire to be intact. It is not the product or even the organization that interests the algorithm of work. It is the production line's infinite curvature. The algorithm of work is a demonstration within a demonstration. With access comes (the necessity of) improvement, which always takes the form of a demand for more access. As the introduction of the consultant inside the organization demonstrates access, so the introduction of the algorithm demonstrates improvement. The algorithm is the machine of self-improvement; as such, it is the only machine that makes new machines. There is a mirror – marking and instantiating self-envisaging's shared exclusivity, that scary, silly, Stuart Smalleyish binary solipsism – that stands between it and man, the only other machine that makes new machines and, in so doing, improves itself. The mirror between man, the mirror, and The Man, man's mirror, is the algorithm. Meanwhile, the inhuman, which is our fleshly inherence and inhabitation in the general mechanics of a general disregard for self-reflection, makes machines because it does not want to improve. Before the algorithm, machines came from strikes, from resistance, from sabotage. Machines made from the algorithm do not wait for the class struggle.

The algorithm of work subjects every labor process on the production line to undoing, disassembly, and incompletion, in order to demand it be completed better, assembled better, done better. It leaves behind not an improved organization but a metric to ensure the organization will never be satisfied. The metric measures everything against its last instance, ensuring that the last instance never comes. The metric demands more access, more measurement of access, more movement, more assembly, more measure of the last instance, which is given in and as enclosure. The consultant is still talking but it does not matter now what he says. The algorithm of work has arrived, algorithmic surplus has gone viral. If the settler could not be heard over the screams of primitive accumulation, and the citizen could not be heard over the noise of the machines, the consultant cannot be heard over the click of the metrics. Mikey heard this noise and walked the other way, another way, so the algorithm could not pass through, so we could hold him up and pass him along.

Chandler reminds us of a term W. E. B. Du Bois invented and employed; "democratic despotism."[21] When the consultant cannot demonstrate access, and therefore the algorithm cannot demonstrate improvement, the consultant calls for policy as once (and still) the citizen calls for heteropatriarchal nationalism or the settler for racist manifest destiny. Policy is past all that, even though all that's not past. Policy comes in to diagnose what's blocking access, and what's blocking access are 'those people.' What's wrong with those people in Detroit who want water, in British Columbia who want land, in Manila who want some place to stay? Policy says there is something wrong with those people that makes it so that the consultant can't get access. But it is the other way around. The consultant is denied access – those people deny him access – because they embrace the general access-in-antagonism that he denies. And so policy must be called. Self-defense becomes the disease. Love becomes the problem because love is the problem, the self-defense of the accessible. But, hey, maybe governance can help, which is to say maybe those practicing self-defense may be willing to self-diagnose, self-reflect, self-improve! One way or another policy will proscribe, or policy will get posed – as democracy, as democratic despotism, where everyone is given the chance to say there is something wrong with those people. Democratic despotism is the imposition of policy and its violent possibilities and impossibilities on the wrong(ed).

Because the thing is, the consultant's not wrong, the algorithm of work is not malfunctioning, the policy hustler is not misdiagnosing. We're wrong, which is why we're wronged. We are incomplete. Moreover, they got the very idea of incompleteness from us! Another word for incompleteness is study, or more precisely, revision. The consultant gets this revision from us, from study, from our sumptuous revisions of one another out of existence, as existence. Study happens and it don't stop. In study, we are engaged consciously and unconsciously. We revise, and then again. This is not just about distinguishing improvement as capitalist efficiency. That is too easy to dismiss. It is about improvement itself, the time-concept, the moral imperative, the aesthetic judgement, which is to say capitalist improvement founded in and on black flesh, its female informality. Revision has no end and no connection to improvement, never mind efficiency.

So the consultant does and undoes institutions but can't access instituted life, can't open black life, can't uncover queer life, can't expose feminist planning around the 'kitchen table' as Barbara and Beverly Smith called it and Tiziana Terranova calls to it again, all noting certain paradoxes of freedom and sequestration in little general intellects of surreal life.[22] He can't access open secrets, can't incomplete what is already incomplete, can't deform what is always informal already, and yet they can't believe and this leads to the state emergency that goes under such names as resilience and preparedness. When democratic despotism fails, simple despotism in the name of democracy must be imposed. Resilience is the name for the violent destruction of things that won't give, won't return to form, won't bend when access is demanded, won't be flexible and (com)pliant. Stopping when you are told to stop and moving along when you are told to move along demonstrates resilience and composure; but broken, breaking, dissed assembly demonstrates itself openly, secretly, dissembling in captured but inaccessible glance, for us, to us, as incomplete and much more than complete. Its daimonic performance can't be individuated and won't be performed.

Hold She

It's not about who's holding you down when you try to jay-walk; it's about who's holding you up. This is the question of hapticality. The police can't hold what's already held. At the same time, what's already held is all that we can hold. That's our haptic institution. Watching mama listen to a song, you're instituted. Here go that Michael Jackson song she turned up to teach me how to dance.

In the photograph, they containerize her, but she is uncontained. They bend her because access and logistics strive to be one. The more she is captured by the police, the photographer, the viewer, the more she is shipped. But the more she is shipped, the more she is held, the more she is handed.

They can't see our hands, and this is demonic to them. The rebelators' hands are held not up to the cops, they are held up to us, holding us up. All hands, all those mouths, must look demonic to them, and queer. It's queer to put yourself in such hands as may come, to be held up by such hands as may reach you.

Just because there are no rules to our access doesn't mean we don't know what to do. We know how to follow a dancehall queen. We know where she study. We hold to where she study. We hold she.

More Than My Damn Self

How can we survive genocide? We can only address this question by studying how we have survived genocide. In the interest of imagining what exists there is an image of Michael Brown we must refuse in favor of another image we don't have. One is a lie, the other unavailable. If we refuse to show the image of a lonely body, of the outline of the space that body simultaneously took and left, we do so in order to imagine jurisgenerative black social life walking down the middle of the street – for a minute, but only for a minute, unpoliced, another city gathers, dancing. We know it's there, and here, and real; we know what we can't have happens all the time.

Our epigraphs bear an analytic of the lost and found, of fallenness and ascension, that comes burning to mind in and as the name of Michael Brown. First, that there is a social erotics of the lost and found in fallenness' refusal of standing. We fall so we can fall again, which is what ascension really means to us. To fall is to lose one's place, to lose the place that makes one, to relinquish the locus of being, which is to say of being-single. This radical homelessness – its kinetic indigeneity, its irreducible queerness – is the essence of blackness. This refusal to take place is given in what it is to occur. Michael Brown is the latest name of the ongoing event of resistance to, and resistance before, socioecological disaster. Modernity's constitution in the trans-Atlantic slave trade, settler colonialism and capital's emergence in and with the self, the state and all the other apparatuses of sovereignty, is The Socioecological Disaster. Michael Brown gives us occasion once again to consider what it is to endure the disaster, to survive (in) genocide, to navigate unmappable differences as a range of (non)localities that, in the end – either all the way to the end or as our ongoing refusal of beginnings and ends – will always refuse to have been taken. The fall is anacatastrophic refusal of the case and, therefore, of the world, which is the earth's capture insofar as it was always a picture frozen and extracted from imaginal movement. At stake is the power of love, which is given, in walking down the street, as defiance to the (racial capitalist, settler colonial) state and its seizures, especially its seizure of the capacity to make (and break) law.

Against the grain of the state's monopolization of ceremony, ceremonies are small and profligate; if they weren't everywhere and all the time we'd be dead. The ruins, which are small rituals, aren't absent but surreptitious, a range of songful scarring, when people give a sign, shake a hand. But what if together we *can* fall, because we're fallen, because we need to fall again, to continue in our common fallenness, remembering that falling is in *apposition* to rising, their combination given in lingering, as the giving of pause, recess, vestibular remain, custodial remand, hold, holding in the interest of rub, dap's reflex and reflection of maternal touch, a maternal ecology of laid hands, of being handled, handed, handed down, nurture's supernatural dispersion. Hemphill emphatically announces the sociality that Luther shelters. Fallen, risen, mo(u)rnful survival. When black men die it's usually because we love each other through objection; it's usually because we are in love, whether we fight or fly, whether fight or flight are held up as surrender. Consider Michael Brown's generative occurrence and recurrence as refusal of the case, as refusal of standing. You can do this but only if you wish to insert yourself, and now we must abuse a phrase of Ah Kee's, into black worldlessness.[23] Our homelessness. Our statelessness. Our selflessness. None of which are or can be ours.

The state can't live with us and it can't live without us. Its violence is a reaction to that condition. The state is nothing other than a war against its own condition. The state is at war against its own (re)sources, in violent reaction to its own condition of im/possibility, which is living itself, which is the earth itself, which blackness doesn't so much stand in for as name, as a name among others that is not just another name among others. That we survive is beauty and testament; it is neither to be dismissed nor overlooked nor devalued by or within whatever ascription of value; that we survive is invaluable. It is, at the same time, insufficient. We have to recognize that a state – the racial-sexual capitalist, settler colonial state – of war has long existed. Its brutalities and militarizations, its regulative mundanities, are continually updated and revised, but they are not new. If anything, we need to think more strategically about our own innovations, recognizing that the state of war is a reactive state, a machine for regulating and capitalizing upon our innovations in/for survival. This is why what's most disturbing about Michael Brown (aka Eric Garner, aka

Renisha McBride, aka Ahmaud Arbery, aka Sandra Bland aka Trayvon Martin, aka Eleanor Bumpurs, aka Emmett Till, aka George Floyd, aka Breonna Taylor, aka Tyisha Miller, aka an endless stream of names and absent names) is our reaction to him, our misunderstanding of him, and the sources of that misunderstanding that manifest and reify a desire for standing, for stasis, within the state war machine which, contrary to popular belief, doesn't confer citizenship upon its subjects at birth but, rather, at death, which is the proper name for entrance into its properly political confines. The prosecution of Michael Brown, which is the proper technical name for the grand jury investigation of Darren Wilson, the drone, is what our day in court looks like and always has. The prone, exposed, unburied body – the body that is given, in death, its status as body precisely through and by way of the withholding of fleshly ceremony – is what political standing looks like. That's the form it takes and keeps. This is a Sophoclean formulation. The law of the state is what Ida B. Wells rightly calls lynch law. And we extend it in our appeals to it.

We need to stop worrying so much about how it kills, regulates, and accumulates us and worry more about how we kill, deregulate, and disperse it. We have to love and revere our survival, which is (in) our resistance. We have to love our refusal of what has been refused. But insofar as this refusal2 has begun to stand, insofar as it has begun to seek standing, it stands in need of renewal, now, even as the sources and conditions of that renewal become more and more obscure, more and more entangled with the regulatory apparatuses that are deployed in order to suppress them. At moments like this we have to tell the truth with a kind of viciousness and, even, a kind of cruelty. Black lives don't matter, which is an empirical statement not only about black lives in this state of war but also about lives. This is to say that lives don't matter; nor should they. It's the metaphysics of the individual life in all its immateriality that's got us in this situation in the first place. Michael Brown lived and moved within a deep and evolving understanding of this:

> if i leave this earth today atleast youll know i care about others
> more then i cared about my damn self....

But we have to consider how, and what it means that, his testament is transformed into an expression of mourning and outrage such as this upon the non-occasion of the non-indictment:

> Go on call me "demon" but I WILL love my *damn self*.

We suffer with but also through this expression of our suffering. For this expression of our disavowal of the demonic – however brutally the police and/or the *polis*, in their soullessness, ascribe it to or inscribe it upon us – is erstwhile respectability's voluntary laying down of arms, its elective demobilization of jurisgenerative force. Meanwhile, Michael Brown is like another fall and rise through man – come and gone, as irruption and rupture, to remind us not that black lives matter but that black life matters; that the absolute and undeniable blackness of life matters; that this is not a judgment of value but a description of a field of activity that obliterates the worldly distinction between the organic and the inorganic. The innovation of our survival is given in embrace of this daimonic, richly internally differentiated choreography, its lumpen improvisation of contact, which is obscured when class struggle in black studies threatens to suppress black study as class struggle.

How much has black studies, as a bourgeois institutionalization of black study, determined the way we understand and fight the state of war within which we try to live? How has it determined how we understand the complex non-singularity that we know now as Michael Brown? It would be wrong to say that Michael Brown has become, in death, more than himself. He already was that, as he said himself, in echo of so much more than himself. He was already more than that in being less than that, in being the least of these. To reduce Michael Brown to a cypher for our unfulfilled desire to be more than that, for our serially unachieved and constitutionally unachievable citizenship, is to engage in a kind of counter-revolutionary brutality; it is to partake in the ghoulish, vampiric consumption of his body, of the body that became his, though it did not become him, in death, in the reductive stasis to which his flesh was subjected. Michael Brown's flesh is our flesh; he is flesh of our flesh of flames.[24]

On August 9, 2014, like every day, like any other day, black life, (con)sent not to be single in irreducible sociality, got caught walking – with jurisgenerative fecundity – down the middle of the street. Michael Brown and his boys: black life breaking and making law, against and underneath the state, selflessly surrounding it. They had foregone the melancholic appeal, to which we now reduce them, for citizenship, and subjectivity, and humanness. That they had done so is the source of Darren Wilson's genocidal instrumentalization in the selfish state's defense. They were in a state of war and they knew it. Moreover, they were warriors in insurgent, imperfect, incomplete beauty. What's left for us to consider is the difference between the way of Michael Brown's dance, its fall and rise, its ongoing nonperformance and the well-meaning protests of mere petitioners, fruitlessly seeking energy in the pitiful, minimal, temporary shutdown of this or that freeway, as if mere occupation were something other than retrenchment (in reverse) of the demand for recognition that actually constitutes business as usual. Rather than dissipate our preoccupation with how we live and breathe, we need to defend our ways in our persistent practice of them. It's not about taking the streets; it's about how, and about what, we take to the streets. What would it be and what would it mean for us jurisgeneratively to take to the streets, to live in the streets, to gather together another city right here, right now?

Meanwhile, against the dead citizenship that was imposed upon them, the body the state tried to make them be, and in lieu of the images we refuse and can't have, here is an image of our imagination. This is Michael Brown, their descent, their ascension, their ceremony, their flesh, their animation in and of the maternal ecology – Michael Brown's innovation, as contact, in improvisation. Contact improvisation is how we survive genocide.

> we didn't get here by ourselves. black takes like black took. we were already beside our selves, evidently. eventually, we were upside ourselves in this wombed scar, this womblike scarring open scream tuned open, sister, can you move my form? took, had, give. because he wasn't by himself he's gone in us. how we got over that we didn't get here is wanting more than that in the way we carry ourselves, how we carry over ourselves into we're gone in the remainder. here, ain't here, bought, unbought, we brought ourselves with us so we could give our selves away. that's more than they can take away, even when its more than we can take.

UNWATCHABLE, UNWATCHABLE

1.
What can't be watched? What violates the idea of security and surveillance, makes this idea unworkable? Short-circuits and overflows and overheats and enrages the watch? This watch chain that allows for policy questions like who watches the watchers. Checks and balances. No, we bounced. The unwatchable are the intolerable. Who does not accede to being watched but turns unwatchable instead? Was always unwatchable but not in relation to the watchable? Never there, never a population, but declare, in violation of being watched, 'watch meh now!?' We, that's who, to more + less than one another, which is us. Who can't you look at? Who you lookin' at, motherfucker? Who'd rather go blind?

2.
Security and surveillance, in all their guises, can't be watched, either. It's not just that we don't want to; it's also that even if we did, they're bound to disappear. Part of why we can't watch that shit is its constant overlooking of what it can't watch, of who won't be watched, us saying "watch me!" to one another being no one in particular. Such overlooking is a brutal form of overseeing. It leaves a trace effect, some residue, the left. It takes up the space it disavows in overlooking like a big ol' gentrifier, a hip settler, the one with the public-private police and the worldly, deictic frame; the one who imagines himself to be

constantly outsmarting himself with certain geometric maneuvers – triangulating, or taking the center, or taking over a school in the name of STEM. The left not only hates the place it takes up but also the people it represents in overlooking and overseeing them. It thinks they are deplorable and, in its dotage, it's stupid enough to say so. Its game of position and removal is where surveillance and disregard converge. You could call this convergence emessenbeseeing but that lets all manner of loud decolonizers of the gentry off the hook. We see you, they say. We're the night watch. You know, artists and shit.

3.

Marx says somewhere that the criminal produces the criminal justice system. So, what does criminality, which is to say we who produce laws made to be broken, produce? Doesn't criminality call order into being with its call to general disorder? Then if we who produce laws made to be broken produce, or perhaps call into being, politics, we necessarily fall before, beyond, and outside of politics. Indeed, we fall, in other words, outside, under, and around the state of exception that is politics' essence and its end. To watch us is to fall into politics; to watch with us is to fall outside of politics with us; it is to fall into our arms. And they could never watch us without falling for us, we who hold them up by holding each other up. Their crush is deadly. They are the refuse that

refuses refuge and visitation. They fall on us when their eyes fall on us. In our fallenness we are befallen by their upright stance. Blackness isn't unwatchable because of whiteness, because whiteness needs it to be, or because whiteness cannot see it; it's not invisible, or surveilled or evaded in dark sousveillance, or exaggerated, or desired; it's not subject to (color) correction even in the total, broken ubiquity of the institution, though the unwatchable may be given all these explanations. Blackness is unwatchable because there's no way to watch it that ain't in it, no way to watch it from the outside, which is to say from its anti-black and worldly effects: politics, policy, legality.

4.

Once there was an artist who was a lawyer. He was demonstrative in his doubleness, always showing himselves making a show of himselves with metaprosecutorial zeal. There was nothing unsettling about it. It was reassuring to the edifice, like a buttress. He only said, 'watch me!' to them and they loved it, saying so through him, his having been encrypted long before he declared the need for secrecy. In this regard, which is disregard, he played an agent from below, and we weren't even there. We don't show up for him when he shows out in uniform. He holds up the one he can't take his eye off and we are indirectly overseen by a leftover, an activist in a hall of mirrors. He overlooks us. He misses all the little differences we feel. Our flesh is ours. His will ain't his. We hand around. He looks away. He can't watch us. We won't watch Him.

AL-KHWĀRIDDIM

Savoir-Faire is Everywhere

THERE IS A RHYTHM MAKING A WORLD, AND THE TIME AND SPACE THIS RHYTHM beats out invites individuation in this world. This is a rhythm that has been around for five hundred years. But now it sounds to itself like the only rhythm, the rhythm of the world, and of the individuals who strive to live in that world. It is the rhythm of commodity production by commodities, internally disrupted at its origin. The first beat renders each commodity separate, bordered, isolated from the next. The second beat renders every thing equal to every other thing. The first beat makes every thing discrete. The second beat makes everything the same. Time and space order this rhythm, and are ordered by it. This is a settler rhythm, this one-two of capitalist production, a rhythm of citizen and subject, of dividuation and individuation, of genocide and law. It sounds out by expropriating any other movement of the beat. It asserts that nothing else can be heard, that nothing else need be felt. It is in short a killing rhythm, as Fanon warned at the end of *Les Damnés de la Terre*. But this rhythm has always been set amidst, and beset by, the general antagonism, the cacophony of beats, lines, falsettos, and growls, of hips, feet, hands, of bells, chimes, and chants, an undercommon track. At the heart of its production is a certain indiscretion, a certain differentiation that will not separate, an unbordered consolation against isolation, a haptical resonance that makes possible and impossible this killing rhythm, the undercommon track that would remain fugitive from the emerging logistics of this deadly rhythm and exhaust it.

Still, today this beating of commodity on commodity insists on a world as never before, wraps its beats around the earth in which the party is compulsory. And it penetrates deep into what did not appear vulnerable or even possible to force into its time and space. Its one-two becomes a zero-one, zero-one as it sorts thoughts, affects, flesh, information, nerves, in ever more precise and minute attributes of duplicate separation. In short, this rhythm becomes an algorithm. Every thing it captures, every thing it invades, every thing it settles is set with a beat that is compelled to hear itself everywhere, feel itself everywhere. This compulsion drives deeper into the bodies it activates, the information it circulates, the nerves it fires to new connections, new networks of discretion and equivalence. Its arbitrage opens this discretion in what was thought to be indivisible, whole, singular, and then opening this discretion closes it in equivalence, clears it for the next beat at the new margins of its rapacious drumming. So, too, does its time and space force every thing into the claustrophobia of its world beat, every thing that is not fugitive is lost.

To be formed is to be formed in this rhythm, to be algorithmically composed, to be compelled to carry this rhythm but also to develop it, to improve it, to export and import it, which is to say that to be algorithmically composed is not just to be beaten but to beat. This beaten beating is what might be called synaptic labor. To answer the compulsion of logistical capitalism it is necessary not just to carry this beat but to improve it, not just to be available to this rhythm but to make this rhythm available, to assail with this rhythm, to prevail in this rhythm against the surrounding informality that unsettles this zero-one, one-two, with a militancy that is neither one nor its absence. What is synaptic labor? It is in the first instance to be opened involuntarily, by compulsion, capriciously, to this rhythm that kills. But this moment of equivalence, of subject embodiment, of exploitable nerve and affect is matched by a degraded discretion, an impulse to take the beating in order to be worthy of holding the whip, an impulse to plot the rhythm upon the earth, to regulate with the rhythm, to form roving beats against fugitive grooves. To improve the land, to make new the people, these old cries uttered over the killing rhythm come back intensively, invasively, internally in synaptic labor, which always begins with administering the beat to one's own rhythm by administering a one to own. The drummer is discrete but indifferent.

The rhythm operates by way of a line. This line is two, zero and one. It is an assembly line where the same is done and the same is improved, as if in courtship with difference, until it is done again. The forwarded email with a comment is the mundane *kaizen* of this rhythm. But this example is deceptive, too, because it is not action but composure, comportment, algorithmic composition that is at stake. Improvement occurs in synaptic labor mostly not through making, but through making more available for exploitation, a primitive accumulation of the senses, and expropriation of intention, attention, and tension. The rhythm operates by way of an assembly line that runs through society, through the social factory, not to make anything in particular but itself. The line of production is its own product. This was the real meaning of kaizen, the improvement of improvement: metrics, algorithmic composition for itself. This means another connection must always be made, and another zero-one opened by that connection. Every connection becomes an arbitrage, every nerve is speculative as it fires in synapsis with another connection, discrete, equivalent, discrete again in nervous metrics of improvement. This metrics is both neurological and pathological in the face of all undercommon measure. And it must pursue such fugitive measure by necessity, by the compulsion to make available and be made available to this rhythm everywhere, all the time, in the where and when of this killing beat.

This is the logistics of algorithmic composition, and the rhythm of logistical capitalism, which envisions and by envisioning envelops and entraps the earth in a world that runs to the end of the earth and is the end of the earth. Logistics runs the globe, runs after the earth and the logisticality that has developed as a capacity on this earth. Logistics extends, expands, accumulates the space and time of a capitalism driven across the earth by the algorithmic zero-one/one-two beat. And by doing so it forces upon the earth, the world. If logisticality is the resident capacity to live on the earth, logistics is the regulation of that capacity in the service of making the world, the zero-one, one-two world that pursues the general antagonism of life on earth. The world is posed as the way to live on the earth as the individual is posed as the way to live in the world. To live in the world as an individual is therefore to be logistic, and to be logistic is to settle into a rhythm that kills, to beat out that rhythm over the undercommon track that keeps (giving away) its own measure. To say that synaptic labor generalizes a certain availability is also to say that insofar as it is derivation, reduction, residuality, it cannot but be less amidst its drive to be more and to improve continuously. And so too for the desperate and dangerous acts of individuation, of global analysis, of policy, of settlement, of a finally imperial antipathy to empathy – a resonance open before it was opened and after it was enclosed.

What one might call the social life of things is important only insofar as it allows us to imagine that social life is not a relation between things but is, rather, that field of rub and rupture that works, while being the work of, no one, nothing, in its absolute richness. Such (social) work is no work at all but the madness remains; rub and rupture all but emerge, but in nothing like an emergence, as something imprecision requires us to talk about as if it were some thing, not just discrete but pure. More specifically, almost salvifically, we want to call it a line, or a pulse, but it won't come. Ani*mate*rial riddim cutting rhythm cutting method – microtonality's overpopulation of measure, *Zaum* preoccupying *Raum* with an extrarational, hyperganjic, dancehallsanskritic, anachorasmiatic, al-Mashic, all mashed up buzz, the alternate groove we in, the devalued and invaluable local insurgency – disobeys our most loving invocation. This gift of spirit gives itself away and zero-one/one-two is left embittered.

The undercommons is not a coalition. It's an absolutely open secret, with no professional ambition. The devaluation of local insurgency takes the form of forgetting, which then manifests itself as mourning for the mass movement that never was, some dreamy coalescence of undishonored ones, a resurrection of this one or that other one that's done gone, like some kind of corporate afterlife. Michael Porter says the fundamental question of strategy is how to get your company out of the market. This exodus takes the form of command, the arbitrary power to make policy but also the regulation and governance of externalities. Policy says: I fixed myself so I can help you. Meanwhile, we squat planning. Don't prove; don't improve; don't even show. This is the romantic dream of the itinerant barbecue. We prepare fire table from oil drum, an immanence (that interinanimation of limit and transgression) always there as something more and less than itself, because the linepulse is so much more and less than that and seems to spread and wonder like a spill, like a neither singular nor plural activity of aggressive bordering or demarcation in (violation of) every locale, everywhere but extraterritorial, in touch but way out, the chic but disenchanted *bons temps* of the shipped, who feel remotely, their afterlife being fleshly and marked by irregular exchange.

Algorithm is the imposition – by rule, at scale – of the impossible task of shared abstraction. Mary Pat Brady shows how scale's bad feel, and the bad feelings the desire for scale requires and induces, are implications of this shared abstraction, this abstracted sharing, this discretionary metaphysics of individuation given in electronic lock step and brutal (single-)line dance as pulse enforcement's networked composition.[25] On all them other hands, algoriddim is contact improvisational violence to the zero-one/one-two, a disruption of its protocols, which form the binary rhythm of the iron system as Adorno accurately described and inaccurately ascribed it. When the senses become theoreticians in their practice a discomposition of the individual occurs; flesh/blackness, as the end/death of the individual, is the individual's decomposition. The move from logistics to logisticality – from forced availability ("in the flesh" as Hortense Spillers puts it) to a mechanics of undercommon hapticality – is, itself, spooky action at a distance, the exterior affects and effects of the intramural. We study the relation between the intramural, as Spillers works it, and entanglement, as Silva works that. They breathe agony into empathy and empathy into ethics and we feel that; they weave difference without separation and we wear that. In the interest of being really useful, we study the minor internal contact and internecine radiation of various quartets, which remain unheard by the ones, you know, the zero-ones/one-twos, who have interests, who are interested in being themselves in the interest of some kind of owning, as if owning were a mode of defense. The only defense is openness. The only owning is unowning. Give everything away until you have nothing. Give it all away until you are nothing. You got to give it up. You can't get ahold of it; you gotta hope, against hope, that it gets ahold of you. That's what the (zero-)ones(-twos) call stealing, when neither self nor world are graspable, which is to say that the closer you get to grasping either one, the closer we get to disappearing. But you already know that everything in blurred lines was already there in got to give it up. In the face of this stealing from the stolen what we continue to receive in them is their stealing away, in undercommon assembly, in the thickness, in varying sharpnesses of drafting and overdrafting, of speculative, anarchitectural, antinational, profanational drawing, of parabolic turns and eccentric, centrifugal, extracircular returns of the drawing of breath, drawn away from it, in and out of itself, off scale, over (and under) rule, (up) against it. Our high-low monastic nothingness is irrectangular blurrrrr, out of line and out of round and out of turn, multiply tabled/terkhed/torqued/twerked/tongued, our uncorralled chorale.

So we crossfade, Zo, where the social skills of the anti-social can't compare to the sociality of the more + less than skilled whose only problem is that they

have no problem. The shit they call social skills is an algorithm for managing anti-sociality. The zero-ones, who can only be where the other ones are, can't compare to the more + less than ones who be everywhere. Sensory processing order is the emergence and hierarchization of things, which is some primitive shit to the more + less than ones who are in the mist, who are the midst, who mix disorder. You the mixer, minor mixmaster in mining, digging with love. We love you don't even begin to say. We think we found each other ain't even close. The overpopulation of the measure. The overcrowding. The forming of the pit. The shaping of the palestra. The non-invasive, unaxed clearing. The subatomic trees. The cosmological feast. The factitious jam. The zero-ones want a pre-given, accountable, measured formula for something that is only worked in provisional, revisional practice where we have no problem, where the problem disappears in precision and impurity, where we must move in measure like a dancer. Man! Even in Eliot, stealing away from certain bankerish tendencies, as if stolen by Olson, even in his phallo-projective embrace of being open(ed), savoir-faire is everywhere![26]

A PARTIAL EDUCATION

Total Education

IS IT NOT THE CASE THAT WE ARE FACED TODAY WITH A TOTAL EDUCATION? THE term comes from Foucault's classic passages on the modern prison regime. Recall that Foucault used the term to speak about the instruction of prisoners in every aspect of daily life and routine. Foucault writes: "It must be the most powerful machinery for imposing a new form on the perverted individual; its mode of action is the constraint of a total education."[27] He further outlines this instruction deployed against perversion:

> In prison the government may dispose of the liberty of the person and the time of the prisoner; from then on, one can imagine the power of the education which, not only in a day, but in the succession of days and even years, may regulate for man the time of waking and sleeping, of activity and rest, the number and duration of meals, the quality and ration of food, the nature and product of labor, the time of prayer, the use of speech and even, so to speak, that of thought...[28]

Now Foucault stressed that because this instruction represented the reform of 'perverted' bodies – bodies that previously had no such discipline – any call for reforming the modern prison was a call for more instruction. Reform produced more instruction. Instruction produced more constraint, or discipline. Discipline only confirmed the underlying perversion of these bodies, and called forth more reform, which called forth more instruction to reform the perversion discipline confirmed. This process is reflected in Foucault's use of the oxymoron "perverted individual," an oxymoron that is nonetheless the source of total education. Perversion violates the principle of the individual by failing to accede to its proper boundaries and comportments, and thus the perverted individual is an ongoing violation that calls total education into being.

In Foucault's account, perversion appears as a turning aside (from the truth) that is, somehow, prior, already existing. A prior turn. An already given turning that requires straightening, that summons reform. Instruction is how we get straightened out insofar as it is how one is straightened out. Correction begins with the ascription of the body itself, the imposition of body onto flesh; the attribution of perversion to the specific body, which justifies its correction, follows from its isolation and manifests itself as the theft of the body that has been imposed by those who assert a right to instruct insofar as *theirs* are bodies that *they* have supposedly both claimed and transcended. The ascription of body, the imposition of bounded and enclosed self-possession, of a discrete self subject to ownership, of ownership activated and confirmed either in theft or trade, might be said to be the first reform, the first improvement, insofar as it is the condition of possibility of reform, or improvement. The assignment of body to flesh is the first stripe of the long, hard, torturously straight, tortuously straightened row. Instruction is the setting in order, the straightening out. Instruction thereby reveals the essential relationship between improvement and impoverishment, between the private and privation at the heart of total education. Perversion's wealth becomes education's profit.

Today there would appear to be few examples of Foucault's total education in prison regimes. The program of reform, the program of prisoner

improvement, has been replaced almost everywhere by one of punishment alone, or what Foucault calls simply the deprivation of liberty. At the same time, in pointing out that the current prison program of 'slow-motion genocide' has long been the global norm in racialized regimes, abolitionist scholars refuse to countenance reform of the exception, alerting us to the fact that reform of the prison *and* reform of the prisoner are as much modalities of genocide as the interplay of privation and privatization that racial incarceration relentlessly innovates.[29] But what if? What if perversion is placed under constraint in the very idea of individuation, which projects improvement's subject as improvement's object? Then the figure of the perverted individual is always already in the system. Conversely, if perversion's location in the individual body is a form of imprisonment and instruction, then perversion is an already given anti-/ante-individuation. If prison/school are two sides of a common institutional structure that operates by way of individuation, then perversion is a pre-carceral breaking out of prison, a pre-scholarly dropping out of school, that continually reveals the ubiquity of the total education that hunts it down and puts it to work. Insofar as it is the case that in prison and in school one's job is to learn, to get it straight, to straighten out, then it is also the case that every citizen and non-citizen, every person and non-person, every worker who is in or out of work – even the enemy combatant, the prisoner, and the supposedly unemployable – is subject to a total education. Indeed, the rampant speculation on improvement made possible today by finance requires an all but universal diagnosis of perversion, a diagnosis that requires instructional methods and institutional structures that are, at once, extremely narrow and hierarchically subdivided. This suggestion may seem to run counter to our common sense about today's price-making market. This market appears to create an atomized landscape that leaves each individual to his or her own devices, free to choose and to act. Indeed, we hear a lot about states that are hollow, and institutions that are dysfunctional. In such a landscape, the idea of a total education requiring a total institution to set it in motion and a totalizing method to set in motion may seem misplaced. Certainly, the assertion that such a total education effectively dominates this landscape appears counterintuitive.

But the idea that we have been left to our own devices, or more technically that we are now responsible for our own social reproduction, needs to be supplemented. We are precisely not left to our own devices. We remain *their* devices both because of and except for *our* perversions, which prompt their constant regulatory and (e)valuative assault in a system in which regulation and valuation constitute and reinforce one another. We are faced with the relegation of perversion to what Silva calls "the equations of value," whose primitive axiom and fundamental operation is individuation.[30] Prior resistance to individuation is both the primary mode of our perversion as well as the structure and activity of persistence that is most essentially productive of value. In this regard, perversion is total education's primary object and justification insofar as all our efforts at social reproduction must be deemed wrong, insufficient, and weak. And, at the same time, all those efforts are capitalized, becoming the engine and the fuel and the object of continuous improvement. It is precisely because of the withdrawal of state and institution from social reproduction that we can be diagnosed as perverted. State and institution withdraw from it, transcend it, separate from it, and in so doing make social reproduction the object of their possessive epistemological and economic grasp. Indeed in many instances the withdrawal itself is now retroactively attributed to our perversions. In other words, without the state and its institutions, how could we be sufficiently regulated and segregated, as a way of achieving and maintaining propriety and securing the freedom found therein? We could not. Then again, maybe, as Etta James says, most of all we just don't want to be free.[31]

We are withdrawn from the state so that the object, in its separation, can be enjoyed. But withdrawal is not truly abandonment; what is at stake, rather, in this withdrawal is a subdivision of enjoyment. What emerges is a kind of homo-socialization (or politicization) of enjoyment – a regulatory straightening and monolithic consumption and de-(en)tangling of enjoyment, as if orgy were constantly replaced by serial monogamy. What separation does to enjoyment is crucial, and cruel. Withdrawal from the object of enjoyment is an act of individuation that is imposed upon that object. More precisely, self-ownership is imposed upon the object as a dormant or etiolated capacity whose ineffectiveness requires that it be submitted to a regime in which it is absolutely subject to being-enjoyed by another. Consider, for example, the imposition upon the enslaved of bodies retroactively and simultaneously declared to be both their own and improperly and ineffectively self-possessed and the concomitant theft of those bodies by the one, The Man, who enslaves. This is the difference between two modes of enjoyment: enjoyment in separation and enjoyment in entanglement; the enjoyment (the use) of (the separable) body and the enjoyment of (entangled or undercommon) flesh. It is for this very reason that instruction is necessary. Instruction is the regulation (for purposes of employment and individual enjoyment) of anoriginal perversion. And because these failures – the constant threat of total system failure as the anoriginal perversion – run across all areas of the social reproduction of life, instruction must also cover all areas.[32] It must everywhere convert failure from a perversion to a point on a line. It must everywhere reduce failure to a bell curve. It must be everywhere. It must be a total education.

The Market Instructs

Today, it is of course primarily the (straightened version of the) market that instructs. It is the market that disposes of our liberty and our time to put itself in the position to offer total education.³³ (If our liberty is disposed of by the state we can be assured that no instruction for reform will be forthcoming.) The first lesson of this total education – after the inevitable diagnosis of perversion (willfully misunderstood as sickness rather than as health) stemming from our deinstitutionalization – is that we must improve. But not just that we must improve, we must improve in every area of life, in all the areas in which we have been abandoned. Our labor, yes, but also our health, our citizenship, our property, our children, our relationships, our tastes. To improve we must be instructed. Instruction begins by making clear that there is nothing wrong with the state, with institutions, or with the market that is not our fault. Instruction requires us to see the straight lines it imagines (in a deeply regulatory modality of imagination as self-picturing, as a picturing of the self-as-one, *Einbildungskraft*) for the sake of a kind of transcendental desire for improvement.

In contrast to the institution, there is something wrong with us because we are never straight enough, never improved enough, recitative in our perversions. And from the perspective of total education, this is not wrong. There is something wrong with us – namely, that we don't wanna be right. This is to say, along with Luther Ingram, that we are in love.³⁴ They want to own, use, and continuously improve (what's wrong with?) us. They seek to impose upon us the perpetual straightening to which they are submitted. Samuel Delany says the normative, which is to say abnormal psychological, model of 1950s homosexuality was that it was a "solitary perversion."³⁵ But this is also, and perhaps more precisely, to say that the institutional judgment of the normal and the abnormal (or, as the artist Arthur Jafa says, the abnormative)³⁶ was in the interest of a submission of perversion, in general, to the solitary for the purposes of its serially solitary ownership, use, improvement, and enjoyment. Indeed any failures in the market, the state, or institutions can be traced back to us. Our improved participation in these entities will improve them. But it will not improve us, at least not enough, because in the end we are the source and sustenance of perversion necessary for total education.

It is we, not society, that are to be reformed, and any critique of society becomes further instruction for us. The reform of any institution under total education is always the reform of us. Everything is wrong with us, and our trouble is that they want what's wrong with us in order to initiate the continual improvement and straightening out of what's wrong with us; this facilitates their imagining themselves somehow to have always already been straight, right, correct. We are the wayward music against which a certain fantasy of straightness will have come into relief, recasting the general as mere background. That fantasy is one among an infinite set that constitutes the general warp and curve and tangle. It is a solitary version of our general perversion, a thing of lightness we must acknowledge ours. The fantasy of dominance and transcendence is dominant and transcendent until we let it go, place it back in the general music of displacement, disallow the severance and detachment that is its essence, recalibrate and celebrate the generality and mutuality of use, enjoyment, feel. Every aspect of us is perverted. Every aspect of individuality can be improved, can be instructed. But because every aspect of us *is* perverted, individuation is imposed upon us in order to make improvement and instruction simultaneously possible and necessary. Every aspect is in need of reform and therefore instruction. The market is concerned not only with "the nature and product" of our labor, but "the time of prayer, the use of speech, and even, so to speak, that of thought."[37] The market does not seek to punish. It seeks to instruct. And since every aspect of us is perverted, instruction must have access to our every aspect. It must have logistical access. It must insist on reforming our bodies to be conduits for the interoperability of work, money, energy, and information. A logistical education means every aspect of us is (to be) a means. Integrated with this improvement in/as all means is the second lesson of this total education. We will fail to improve enough. We will always need improvement and we always will.[38] Another word for this second lesson is speculation.

The market joins forces with the state and its ideological and repressive apparatuses in this second lesson. Indeed in many instances it is the state that makes the diagnosis of perversion, and in every instance the state that secures the market. The state returns to its settler roots securing not just private property but the private individual, indeed securing individuation itself as a principle necessary for speculation of this kind. Maria Josefina Saldaña-Portillo teaches us how property rights were foisted on indigenous people not only to extract land but also to instantiate individuation as the basis of the settler state's expansion and legitimation.[39] Incessant privatization of social production, policing, property rights, and propaganda remain the state's specialties in this regard. But the state also joins the instruction in improvement, and in particular the speculative market in improvement. As a brief example, think of gentrification. To experience gentrification is to be instructed in speculation. One must learn to see history, parks, schools, natural environments, cultural difference, health, and public life all as monetized values that can be bet on, or against. These contemporary pilgrims want to 'bring the neighborhood up.' They desire its improvement, which means they also desire that which is to be improved. They detach themselves from, or exile, that which is to be improved and that detachment remains the essential structure of their desire. That's why gentrification, as a force, is always seeking after the next neighborhood to conquer. It's a Lacanian cheap trick, as it were. They not only want that which is to be improved, they also want to be wanted by that which is to be improved, desired by perversion. Crime, failing schools, disused or misused parks, and public transportation are subjected to the diagnosis of perversion. And the diagnosis is carried out by citizens. Citizens of gentrification take over schools, clean parks, work with the police, and generally identify those with something wrong with them. This conduct of oneself as a citizen of gentrification has as its schoolmaster this speculative state. To be instructed in gentrification is however not just to subject others to evaluation for improvement but also oneself. It is to submit to self-diagnosis, testing one's capacity for improvement in the form of more speculation, such as the ability to take on more debt, more lifelong learning, more flexibility, more subservience to this speculative market in improvement. As degrading as this self-diagnosis may be, it is preferable to being diagnosed by those who self-diagnose, better, in other words, than being the ones who are said by others to have something wrong with them. It's better to say something is wrong with me than it is to have them say there's something wrong with you. It's better to straighten yourself out.

Usufruct's Modernity

This regime of improvement might be said to have its origins in modern *usufruct*. Usufruct is a term that signals the coming together of two kinds of improvement at the beginning of the nineteenth century. On the one hand, the bourgeoisie had been championing the possibility, and necessity, of improving oneself, in contrast to the static status of the aristocracy. On the other hand, the growing imperatives of colonialism and capitalism to find investment meant that all land and all people became judged by how much more they might improve, how much more they might yield and *should* yield from investment. What is truly sinister about this social synthesis is that it reinforces the fictitious idea of the self-improving, self-owning, self-authoring individual precisely through the act of positing the unproductive and under-willed land and people that surround this fiction, which requires massive resources to sustain itself, producing the impoverishment it posited by means of *individuated* dispossession in the service of ownership. Thus, the supposed independent will of the 'usufructuary,' the one who improves someone else's property, having penetrated will's relative absence in the 'naked owner,' is destined to dominate, to improve, to instruct the other. One could argue that this has also been the basic model of the formal education systems that subsequently developed. Another word for it is marriage.[40]

So we might well ask where this grim picture of compulsory improvement – culminating today in total education – leaves those who traditionally have been classed as instructors: the parent, the teacher, the artist, and the movement leader. We would say it leaves them at study. Study perverts instruction. Study emerges as the collective practice of revision in which those who study do not improve but improvise, do not develop but regenerate and degenerate, do not receive instruction but seek to instantiate reception. Study is our already given gift of the *general* dispossession of ourselves for each other, and our service to that dispossession. Study is the (im)permanently unformed, insistently informal, underperforming commitment to each other not to graduate but instead indefinitely to accumulate an invaluable debt to each other rather than submit ourselves to their infinitely fungible line of credit. Study is a partial education.

Partial Education

Partial education begins with a frank perversion of a frankly Maoist formulation. His formulation is the one becomes two; ours is that the one becomes more and less than that. This indigent refusal of the integer, this violation of number's wholeness, is the first antagonism of a partial education, the opening partisan move. The first action in the practice of a partial education is to say the total education with which we are faced is not total, not one, but more and less. And if it is more or less more and less, then this means some part of it does not belong to it. It belongs to us, and therefore no one and all. To say total education is (not one) is to say we are not just faced with critiquing their instruction, but that we are also at study, and that, insofar as this is true, we ain't studying them. A partial education also insists on the asymmetry of this formulation. Our thing is fundamentally unlike their thing, because our thing is unfounded, ungrounded, undercommon. A partial education is never ready, never started or finished, underfundamental and unsound(ed). It is destined to be unfinished and undone. A partial education is an incomplete education undertaken by we who are incomplete, to borrow Robinson's ante-seminal, ante-sermonic formulation in *The Terms of Order*.[41] A partial education is practiced by the parts that are more and less than themselves, so much so as to continually generate much ado. A partial education is a perversion of instruction. Invaginatively, it plays out the irreducible interplay of usufruction and instruction.

A partial education is also not a neutral education designed to be rightly whole, total, and thereby to replace the bad total education we now face. Its concern is not with replacement but with displacement. A partial education is the partisan point of view of no point of view. It insists on how what is ours is more and less than that. A partial education is a partisan brigade that calls forth the general antagonism in its distinction about what it is not, and what it is. In other words, while a partial education is an antagonistic education, it is also more and less than that in what Silva teaches us to call its inseparable differences.[42] It moves against the grain of the taxonomies, categories, and identities of total education set forth by the usufruct of the European Enlightenment. A partial education is a sensual education, a sensate education. It is a synesthetic theory of the senses, after the fact of the senses having become theoreticians in their practice.[43] A partial education *spills* its own senses – as Alexis Pauline Gumbs's term turns loose.[44] A partial education proceeds and recedes by its own spills.

Gumbs's work is inspired by Spillers, just as the concept of a partial education is inspired by the way Spillers calls into question the oneness both of capitalism and its most insightful critique, Marxism.[45] This critique, never mind its object, requires that there be some distance between the commodity and the laborer, no matter how small or how threatened with collapse into each other, for 'politics' to exist. Spillers, like Robinson, teaches us in effect that even this one, Marxism, is more and less than that because the commodity that could speak is an antagonism internal to that irrevocable antagonism to capitalism, and for this reason may carry something more and something more partial than politics.[46] By implication, then, this critique embodied particularly in the slave woman, and continually fleshed out by her under the most brutal conditions of what Hartman calls "burdened individuality," is also a critique of politics itself and therefore of the very idea of the state, as we can perhaps see in the artists discussed below.[47]

The Singapore Model

In 2015, Singapore's Prime Minister Lee Hsien Loong said in an interview with CNN, "People say we are paranoid which I suppose we are and we need to be."⁴⁸ He was widely ridiculed for a remark that sounded like a throwback to Singapore in the 1970s and 1980s, when his father ruled the country with an even more authoritarian grip. But in fairness to the younger Mr. Lee, he was speaking about the pressure Singapore felt to remain competitive in a world where globalized firms and international finance limit the traditional role of developmental states like Singapore. Nonetheless, the comment was symptomatic, because harkening back to an earlier era of instruction in the nation-state. Singapore emerged precisely as a 'model' through its claim to make citizens who were less perverse. Singapore did this by ruling pretty much everything inside the country as perversion, *except* wage labor and compulsory savings, deference to state power, and heteronormative family life. But Singapore also did this by instructing its citizens that even more grotesque perversity lay all around the island nation, from the enemy within, such as those of Chinese descent, who might be allied to the communists in Malaysia or in China, to the religious fanatics submerged below the surface in a sea of Islam surrounding the secular nation-state, to common criminals lying in wait should Singaporeans travel abroad. Even today, the first thing one hears as a visitor from a local taxi driver is how safe Singapore is – as if one could never survive a walk through Bangkok, or Jakarta, or Hanoi, without encountering bandits.

Contrary to the stereotype, even many Singaporeans often saw through these very visible attempts at instruction, and for this reason the Singapore model was not truly a model of total education. It was not the bodies and souls of Singaporeans that were trained, but merely their public manners – their comportment as citizens, more than subjects. Even today, awkward public education campaigns, like Mr. Lee's comment, remain an anachronistic feature of this kind of straightening of the Singaporean into citizenship. But although Mr. Lee had the wrong kind of instructor's manual in his hand, he had the right concern about continuous improvement in Singapore today. Singapore is subject to a new regime of usufructuary. And with it a new kind of total education in Singapore is emerging, one led by the global economy, with the government scrambling to update its curriculum to keep up. Indeed, today Singapore is a prime example of bodies being instructed logistically by the global economy. With its dominant sectors of finance, hospitality and travel, retail, and health and education leading the way, a new kind of instruction in access is emerging that would be invasive even for Foucault's prisoners. Total education is taking the form not so much of a speculative improvement, but a logistical one. With most people in Singapore living in government housing, and class mobility severely constrained, it is logistics, not finance, that most characterizes the education of the population in this financial center. The Singapore 'model' helps us to understand how we might understand the way in which a logistical instruction operates as a general degradation of means.

With this instruction, the body is to become a means only for the smooth flow of transactions. It is to become a means for the interoperability of all things. Instruction is given in opening the body through such discourses and practices as customer service, prosumer behavior, and indeed in financialization of the self, as Randy Martin put it, but most of all endless availability, 24-hour access, to every aspect of the body.[49] Even the exhortations to creativity, criticality, and entrepreneurship chiefly train the body for the extension of access into social life, imagination, and cultural knowledge. The body is instructed in becoming a means to these flows above and below the level of its integrity as body, to these connections that source new planes of intellect and affect. But always this training is in/as a means to the transaction, to accumulation, to the realization of private profit from social production. Capital seeks only the degradation of means and cannot abide what Malcolm X understood as an end when he uttered his famous phrase "by any means necessary." Not any means but only those that serve capital's limited imagination, that is to say only those means that can be degraded through individuation, through placing freedom above necessity.

Logistical instruction, the new total education in Singapore, allows us to understand the government's latest paranoid attempts to aestheticize its curriculum and move beyond the crude 'rote learning/no cane no gain' approach of its state-led industrialization.[50] Still this total education in logistics cannot but reveal the new perversions on which it thrives, perversions that are at the same time very old in the region. This total education is indeed symptomatic of the perversion of the Singapore model, which is to say its basis and its baseness. These perversions threaten the wealth of the city because that wealth depends on them, a dependency. We will return to this.

Marx predicted that the flows of capital would become part of the production process. We find this prediction in full effect in the work of Anna Tsing, who even demonstrates the dominance of such flows in many sectors, including many of the sectors prominent in Singapore's economy.[51] Developing a capacity of being not just open to others, but opened by others, to be parted, parceled, sent, shipped is to develop what we have elsewhere called *logisticality*.[52] Logisticality is the perversion of logistics, which again is to say its formless fount. A logistical education responds to this underflowing, undercommon logisticality. It attempts to straighten out – that is degrade – this pervasive perversity of access, of vulgar openings. It must respond to a reversal of the first reform – the imposition of the body on the perversion of flesh. Logistics treats the body partially, accessing parts, disaggregating parts, leaving parts behind. It is therefore crucial that logistics not lead to the kind of partial education where such perversity – of flesh without integral bodies, of bodies entangled with flesh rather than housing it – might re-emerge as a form of study among those who want to be accessed because they want to be wrong.

Logistical Perversions

The arts can help here. Or rather the art market, the art scene, the art experience, as Singapore has both imported and created them. The opening of the Gillman Barracks signaled the Singapore government's commitment to making the island nation-state a hub of contemporary arts. The Gillman Barracks, a colonial-era military facility spread across several lush acres in the west of the island, was refurbished to house numerous small private art galleries, restaurants, and the Centre for Contemporary Art, the public institution anchoring the redevelopment. Shortly thereafter, the Singapore Museum of Modern Art opened its doors in the colonial-era supreme court building, now housing modern art of the region from the twentieth century, providing the patrimonial credentials for the push into the world art market. Indeed the clear market strategy of investment in the arts is apparent in the way Singapore Art Week, a massive commercial show held in the iconic Marina Bay Sands buildings on the harbor, has eclipsed the Singapore Biennial, housed in a colonial-era orphanage: although recently this former orphanage, now the Singapore Art Museum, has closed for upgrades. Through these institutional vehicles, and through residencies, publications, grants, university programs, and smaller festivals, the Southeast Asian artists, curators, critics, and collectors have been drawn in substantial numbers to this golden hub. A contemporary art scene has been incorporated into the Singapore model. Singaporeans are to receive a total education in art.

But in what are they to be instructed? Art theory? Investing in the art market? The value of art as social practice? Well, indeed all of these. In a country as wealthy as Singapore, where one quarter of households is said to have over one million US dollars in disposable income, a bit of art theory in the form of instruction from curators, academics, critics, and gallerists will grease the wheel of art market investment, and perhaps social practice will step in when the wheel runs over someone. Singapore Art Week included in its catalogue a buyer's guide that instructed potential investors not to buy undiscovered artists over fifty years of age, since they are at that point unlikely to be discovered and become a good investment, or alternatively to wait until they die to buy them, since posthumous discovery is also a market strategy.

But most of all, on display in the Gillman Barracks private galleries, at the Singapore Biennial, and during the Singapore Art Week is an aesthetic lesson bound to logistical education. Art will shore up the integrity of the Singaporean at a time when logistics cares not for such individuation. It will allow for persistence of individuation, just as speculation does, at the moment things are falling apart, to parts, toward a partial education. This moment remains necessary not just for instruction and improvement, but for realization itself, for scythe of privatization of social production, and the hammer of privation. At a time when logistics takes some emotions and leaves others, groups some of our tastes with tastes of others, lines up our desires with others, merges our criticism with others, art can teach us that we still have boundaries, still have bodies to be constrained, still have individual judgment. The aesthetic lesson, itself a marriage of flesh and body consummated by a higher faculty, is the part of the curriculum designed to put a break on our logisticality, designed to break our logisticality. In other words, it is through the aesthetic lesson that Singapore will seek to secure individuation amid a broader logistical education that must flirt with logisticality. But will we learn the lesson? Or will we continue to fall to pieces in/as our study, in our perverse, partial education? A partial answer for those who would seek to pervert instruction can be found in two of the artists at the Singapore Biennial.

Marta Atienza and Hemali Bhuta

Two installations supposed to be integral to this emerging aesthetic education in Singapore, one by Marta Atienza, an artist from the Philippines working in Rotterdam, and one by Hemali Bhuta, an artist from India, instead fell apart from this total.[53] Both were extraordinarily powerful and beautiful works. Amid a typical contemporary biennial, orderly and ordering of artists, nations, curators, and spectators, something perverse is in the works, in their works. The biennial produces a tour with integrity of individuated countries, art works, artists, opinions, judgments, and sales. By the end of an art world version of a Lonely Planet trip we are to be restored for further instruction in logistics. But Atienza and Bhuta do not take part in this tour. They part from it, depart from it, and from themselves too. Itineraries drop into parts in the presence of their work. We forget where we were going, our senses filled with being where we are. Atienza's work fills a room and – like Bhuta's – spills out at us before we reach the room down a small hall. We hear the sea. Her installation consists of a kind of deck onto which water spills, a porthole that moves up and down on the horizon, half submerged by the sea, and a series of watery projections. We learn that she took a ride on a tanker, the kind plying the waters around Singapore. We learn she has connections with Filipino sailors who work these tankers. To be in the room is to have our sense of the sea disassembled. We can hear it and see it, and we feel we should be able to smell it and touch it. the isolation of sound and sight renders us partial. We cannot put ourselves together, can't pull ourselves together in this seascape. Something is wrong and it is us.

Bhuta's installation is also reached before we arrive. The air forms a scented path. The viewer follows the path and turns to see a thicket of hanging incense, hung delicately from the ceiling but heavily too, like it would be hard to push aside and easy to become entangled. The red forest is textured by the rough growth of each incense stick and it is hard to know if this surface is soft or sharp, safe or dangerous. But most of all the scent occupies us, a silent scent we dare not touch. As with Atienza's work, we are affected, again to use a term from Silva.[54] The senses lose composure and we lose a bit of self-possession. We become partial. Ferreira da Silva writes about the denigration of the affectable ones in early Enlightenment Europe, those who are not fully self-owning and self-defining, but are affected, undone, made incomplete, made partial by others. Both pieces allow us to feel the dispossession of partiality, the mere part. There is an excited feeling of wanting to be with others in this art.

These two works by female artists from the Philippines and India could instead have engaged in critique, like a number of artists appeared to do in the Biennial and at Art Week. They could have questioned the exploitation of Filipino sailors under Singaporean flags, of Filipina domestic workers locked in the homes of Singapore's middle class, of South Asian construction workers indebted and injured building Singapore's mega-projects, of the skin-color racism still hurled at South Asian children in Singapore school yards. Indeed there were several other pieces that referenced the housing condition of migrants from South Asia, and sounds of the city filled with the voices and languages of its migrants. These two artists would likely have also been included in the Biennial for such gestures. After all, reform requires Singapore to confront international newspaper headlines like "Buy a discount maid at Singapore's malls," or simply and commonly "Singapore's Migrants Face Abuse and Resentment."[55] The arts would then clearly be instructing us in a misalignment. And indeed they would be making the case for reform, for more instruction, and ultimately for more art. But their art is far more partisan than this.

Non-State Non-Being

A partial education does not produce citizens who think this way because it does not produce anything as complete as a citizen, but something much more perverse. In the craft of these artists one is instead encouraged to become entangled with not-citizenship, with not-state being. One begins to feel the migrant workers not as slighted citizens, but as part of another tradition of partisanship, of cultural experiment, and of perversion in the face of the citizens, nations, and states that would claim them. Not by coincidence the region has in fact a rich history of this perverse notn-statism as James C. Scott teaches us in *The Art of Not Being Governed*. In describing the vast regions of what he calls Zomia, highlands and remote regions that extend from India through mainland Southeast Asia to Southern China, Scott speaks of peoples who not only live without states, but develop strategies to avoid being incorporated into those states, to avoid being "in-gathered." Scott notes that these peoples were often known in the language of those who hunted them, those who lived in states, by the word in those state languages for 'slave,' even before they became enslaved, signed a previous perversity. Scott's work gives us an historical context for contemporary diplomatic citizenship, and the partial education that confronts it. He writes about Southeast Asia:

> Paraphrasing an observation by Karl Marx about slavery and civilization, there was no state without concentrated manpower; there was no concentration of manpower without slavery, hence all such states, including especially the maritime states, were slaving states... Slaves, it is fair to say, were the most important "cash crop" of pre-colonial Southeast Asia: the most sought-after commodity in the region's commerce.[56]

And this is not just a context for our present discussion but, together with European colonial indenture, *the* historical context of the Singapore model:

> Another way of describing the process is the systematic removal of captives from non-state spaces, particularly, the hills, in order to deposit them at, or nearby, state spaces... The scale of slaving and its effects are hard to imagine... whole regions were stripped of their inhabitants...
>
> As is so often the case with a major commodity, slaves became virtually the standard of value by which other goods were denominated – the tight association between hill peoples and the social origin of most slaves is strikingly indexed in the fact that the terms for slaves and hill peoples were often interchangeable.[57]

Moreover, because it is so recent, this maritime state, Singapore, may appear to be the product of more recent colonial-era indenture. Indeed from Chinese *kongsi* (big brothers) indenturing laborers from Fujian, and addicting them to opium, to the British indenturing the Tamils on rubber plantations, to the displacement of Malay peoples on the island, this modern nation-state might appear to be only the product of the movement from subject to citizen in the post-colonial era.[58] Although inserted into a racial hierarchy, working-class Chinese, Tamils, and Malay peoples all became Singaporeans upon independence. But, with the help of Atienza and Bhuta, with the benefit of a partial education, the one-off post-colonial citizenship soon becomes more than one and less than two, and something partial, something non-state, something echoing the legacy of Zomia emerges. Because Singapore has come to require precisely that "concentration of manpower" that the slaving states required. And this raises the question not of what Singaporeans call those who must be "in-gathered" so much as what the in-gathered might come to call themselves, so much as their own ungathered, split practices of the partial.

At any given moment there are roughly five million people in Singapore. Three million are citizens, legacies of the subject to citizen history, together with a policy of *sinification* that has encouraged post-independence migration of those of Chinese descent. The rest are migrants, most on two-year work visas, working as domestics, in construction, and in all forms of maintenance, repair, and physical upkeep of the world city. A small portion of these are on longer work visas, and are called expats, and are mostly white. In other words, bringing in concentrated manpower remains the model of the state. It is not now a slaving state, though Singapore continues to be a regional hub for trafficking women and girls. It does, however, regulate an economy that produces massive numbers of indebted to the point of indentured South Asian male workers, and one that produces new runaway domestic workers every day of the calendar year. The scale of the dependence on this concentrated manpower, the widespread dehumanization of those in-gathered, and the utter dependence of the Singapore model on this manpower turns the one of total education into two. It is not so much that these migrant workers are misaligned with their nations and states, as Singapore is misaligned with itself. Its model is perverse. It presents itself as a model of Southeast Asian development. But it is present to itself as a perversion.

Given Derangement

What does not and can never belong to these workers is a model that exhibits the worst of both entwined histories – the pre-colonial model of sweeping up non-state peoples through violence, and today through debt, deceit, and development, and the colonial model of European racism. This latter model means that these workers will never be considered potential Singaporean citizens, as they probably would have become 'padi-state' subjects under pre-colonial slaving states. We have in-gathering without the prospect of citizenship. The colonial regimes stained the region with a form of racism that allows post-colonial regimes to choose the worst of both worlds. This is the actual Singapore model. Not free market but massive concentrations of unfree labor. Little wonder it can be extolled, sold, but not copied. What other nation-state could in-gather and exclude with such ferocity without raising the ire of its own substantial impoverished population? None. Not even Singapore.

But from our point of view, which is the refusal of a point of view that partial education makes more fully operative, this last question and reality of the Singapore model in general is precisely their thing, not ours. What spills out from the perverse splitting in two of this model, of this total education, are the parts we might care about. Atienza and Bhuta do not instruct us in aesthetic individuation. Their works cannot be reformed. Their partiality stands with us in antagonism to reform, to instruction. The sea, the air, the spirits that carry these beings gathered by Singapore in, but not of, its model spill out in an irreconcilable critique of state life, of citizenship, of the individual body. Their presence in the state is a refutation of the state as universal form, as total education. And in the uncoercive re-arrangement of the senses – to swerve with Spivak's term – these works allow us to ask what perversions might already be here and now.[59] Those who sojourn derange their senses for others, who offer to pervert us. And without the state to order them into citizens, these dispossessed senses form the baseless, found education of another kind: a turning to our partial versions.

INDENT

(To Serve the Debt)

First Layer

WITH GRADUAL EMANCIPATION, IN MANUMISSION'S INTERMINABLE ARC, WHICH Patricia Ann Lott brilliantly analyzes, you become responsible for your financialization.[60] You become accountable, discounted, devalued, envalued. Black history is the theory of the subject's exhaustion. Black history is the subject's exhaust. From the non-perspective of that fucked-up after-party, gradual emancipation is the subject's interminably terminal condition. The opposite of freedom is freedom. The Brown Buffalo teaches us that gradual emancipation is what it is to be chained to that struggle. Gradual emancipation is not isolated to the northern states, as an antebellum exception; nor is it the bind or bond exclusively proper to the enslaved, to their lives or afterlives. Hartman teaches us that it is the general rule that structures human freedom as subjection. This has to do with what Frederick Douglass begins to refer to under the rubric of "plantation peculiarity." But it isn't just residual servitude, or servile affect; it's a certain (self-)consciousness with regard to that affect that turns out to be the essence of political animality. You could speak of it as shame, which tries to assert itself as superior to the behavior that induces it. Shame is what accrues to manumission. It is the imposition of credit, of the requirement to pay a debt to society's antisociality, a requirement internalized as 'freedom.'

Manumission is, in every way, never enough. Its calculation loses meaning and exactitude. We have to look away or look awry.

The general abstraction is like the El gone underground. Poetic detachment is public transportation – a social force, or a popular campaign, or a populous expedition. It's not a team but it is a kind of teeming, an inappropriable swarm having a funky and inappropriately good time, dispersed as an infinite series of breaks in an infinite passion. Abandon in abandonment can't be read in any other way. If you're stranded and you can't go home, or can't get out, then you have to go farther away and further out. If you're fallen and you can't get up, all you can do is get down until you pierce the bottom of the broken world and its infinite crises in and out of regulation. So you ground, knowing that it's necessary but insufficient, until exhausted; with neither world enough nor time, earth be present and been gone. Ascension comes to those who dig, without global position, in turned, anaproprioceptive descent, a common insurgency you twist and shout, as how you remain, as how you stay. To stay *there*, in a constant rehearsal of being sent from there into there's other plane as there's other plain, is to place not just this or that concept of this or that object into question; it is, rather, to place the concept as such under an intense generative and degenerative distress. Black study is just this extraconceptual or anaconceptual force, counter-negative propulsion written in duplicate on the same sheet, cut along a jagged line, serrated, winding, a chirographic dance up to the instrument and through it, a solo so multiple, an instrument so deeply and habitually prepared, an indenture so commonly disbursed, an abstraction so dispersively sown, that even financialization falters. It can neither be insured nor secured. It's like it has been played so hard that tuning is other than what it is, like tuning is illuminated, like a contract for destruction and rebuilding that can only be fulfilled in something both more and less than performance. Everything's written together, huh? We anticipate and survive being torn apart.

To read Spillers's "Mama's Baby, Papa's Maybe: An American Grammar Book" alongside her "The Crisis of the Negro Intellectual: A Post-Date" is to know and love this: that black study is (about) the production of concepts only insofar as it is something like a preconceptual or postconceptual, generative differentiation of concepts (some kind of excessive inhabitation of the concept's material meta- or anastatic division and collection *in the flesh*); it is a way, out of no way, through the conceptual field, not because the conceptual is originary but because the conceptual founds the regulative response to the anaconceptual thing that has no name. When Spillers says the black woman would have had to be invented if she had not already existed (which also moves in her ongoing subtle push against and through Fanon), was she saying that the black woman – as commodity, as instrument, as tool, as machine – is a star? This is the most horrific of all possible double edges: to be crypt and cryptograph, to (dis)embody the concept as underconceptual flesh. And so we say that black study is violence in and toward the concept that is, as it were, before the concept. It is the underprivileged living of that violence, divine because it's so goddamn low, given in a metaeconomics of gift and disrupted givenness. Black study is a ministry of profanation, a public house of earthy devotion. Black study is the fruit of the service tree. Black study is out of my star. Black study is out from fallen stars.

When J. Kameron Carter takes up the question concerning the "God-terms" that underwrite sovereignty, he shifts it and us so that we really start thinking, also, about the "Man-terms" that underwrite sovereignty as well.[61] He works a kind of persistent cosmological inconstancy, with a dark energy that anticipates the unfixing of the stars that it follows, allowing us to have to ask why man became God as if it were before the question of why God became man; now we get to have to ask how it is that becoming God is tantamount to what Gayle Salamon calls, "*assuming a body.*"[62] What is it to assume, to conceptualize, to take up and take onto oneself a body? What is it for the body and the self to take one another up and take one another on in serial preface to each, in the other, being taken out? What remains beyond that address, that incursion, that aggressive vulnerability, that brutally projective and protective settlement, which is sovereignty in the midst of its diffusion? Meanwhile, mutiny, the general strike, the remorseless working of no-things and no-bodies, romantic comedy in the commons, its antinomian swerve and quarrel, living's dissolute spread, its dispersive largesse, its cosubstantial blur, its transubstantial fade, can't be faded, requiring that we speak, maybe appositionally, to some insubstantial pageantry of the anasubstantial. Are substance and sovereignty so bound up with each other (substance being an unreal matter of *having* mass and *occupying* space in time, on time's line) that we have to imagine a more improperly surreal physicality? Not anti-matter but ante- and after-matter. Maybe flesh is matter's Auntie, matter's play mama, who survives having and occupying. So that what's at stake is the necessity of a more emphatic analysis of flesh, as something other than withdrawn or withheld or reduced body, as that which is, therefore, apposed to body. One wants to speak (of) (through) (as) flesh in its own terms; but flesh has no terms, though the terms that are imposed upon it become its interminable preoccupation with cœnobitic commotion.

Second Layer (Parts 1 & 2)

Because some folks have been asking about the concept of the undercommons, we have decided to try to talk a little bit about the undercommons of the concept. Black study moves against the mastery of and over the concept as if it were a matter of life and death. But more important, black study means you serve your concepts without a master(y). And this would mean that the rupture of subjection and objection is never closed, healed, settled for plunder and expropriation. This is why those who master concepts hate black study so much, in what appears to be a disproportionately violent response to its service. They can't stand it because serving something without a master is a totally open form of love.

Somebody said they were reading a Toni Morrison novel and were amazed how the lives, the mere experiences, of the characters reminded them of Alfred North Whitehead's concept of prehension. To recognize that Whitehead stands for any theorist you want is to embark upon the drafting of a script. So, here we go, in the anteroom of the concept, just out of reach, trying to get a grip, waiting to become objectified, hoping to become another for an other. Again and again, in carceral luxury, maybe at a gallery, or in the faculty club, or in somebody's studio, where authentication is always just on the other side, where objects are always falling back against the undercommon thing, as if the chamber tilts them away from whatever is supposed to be behind the curtain they've almost been caressing, we strain against what it is to be incapable of having an experience. Prospective others want some body, need a body, so they can be Somebody. Looped, vicarious, oscillating between precarity and security, we're concerned with what it means to be concerned with the meaning of Somebody saying you are nothing but mere experience. Meanwhile, who wants to embrace the undercommon experientiality that accrues to the refusal of what it is to have? No-body does. Black study – the fugitive activity of mas(querading) as mere, as pure, experience – is no-body's radical empiricism, held in the question of the meaning of living behind lives that are said to be in need of explanation, in want of conceptualization, in search of self-possession. The living of mere experience is terrible in the richness of its making.

Deleuze says we don't yet know what a body can do. Can we imagine what we don't know that flesh can do? Because flesh won't do, it does. Flesh senses extra while, with the transatlantic slave trade, capital 'invents' a collectivization of broken, working 'bodies.' Such invention, such bad sociological finding, can't know that flesh was working, sensing, before capital and its concepts got there. Capital wants to master that mystery, but the incalculable is invaluable no matter how much you count it, no matter how many times you put a price on it, no matter how regularly and regulatively you lock it up or shoot it down. At the same time, the liability imposed upon us, our incorporation into the regime of credit in an absolute and brutal injunction to remit, is immeasurable and endlessly to be paid. They assign a value to the invaluable; they give it terms. And, *because the case for reparations has been made against us*, we are required to pay those terms, which cannot correspond to our value because we are invaluable, but rather conform to a conceptualization of the invaluable (which is all value ever is), given in and as mastery, as its attempt to grasp mystery, to capitalize indenture, to steal the debt we are supposed to serve.

Harriet Jacobs teaches us that because we are invaluable, we can never pay for ourselves. Nevertheless, we are required to pay. Incessantly we pay what can't be paid. We pay, and pay, and pay, but not to own. Even our mothers, even our children, are not ours. We never come to terms, and this is too terribly beautiful for words. Our indebtedness is all we have, and all we have is what we owe to 'one another.' It's what we hand, and feel, as feel, in the defiance we pay to payment, and credit, and mastery, until one and another fail to signify, until they are absolutely nothing, until one and another are no-bodies. That indebtedness is what we live, is the living we make, as the invaluable. The impossible and impossible-to-satisfy master is dazzled by it, would open it, wants total access to it, but what they do in the absence of that access, which will have been endured as enclosure, is conceptualize it, place a value on it, impose terms upon it that are meant to approach and explain and regulate the invaluable, the incalculable, while also submitting it to the wasteland of credit, the outer depths of usury, the desert, the slough, the plantation, the prison of the eternally payable, the interplay of segregation and pursuit in genocide that manumission and enlargement surreptitiously intensify.

Here's how we're supposed to pay our debt to society: Master, this is who you are; Master, this is where you are; Master, this is when you are. He's always asking us to tell him who he is; this motherfucker won't leave you alone. We pay him his identity, his place, his time, and all he can do is wonder, viciously. Voraciously, he wants to close the question. Because ceaseless accumulation is a poor substitute, he wants to close the book that won't stop talking. He can't keep thinking that it talks to him through us. He wants to think it's gonna say for sure. We have to keep rehearsing what the book says; it's never gonna say the final word. Sovereign musclehead. Predatory lender. Ship-circler. Mad scientist. Great white captain shark. Olaudah Equiano lived it before Georg Wilhelm Friedrich Hegel thought it, torture and miracle, to serve without a master in mastery's ugly fucking face.

Robinson teaches us that black study necessarily precedes and at the same time has to wait not only on the concepts it serves, but also on the concepts that attempt to master it, which will come only well after it, and will keep coming after it, with everything they got. Consider, as the most fateful example, Foucault's mistake, though it is others who turn this mistake into such a stake. He writes – inaugurating his interest in biopower and, by extension, governmentality – of "the adjustment of the accumulation of men to that of capital, the joining of the growth of human groups to the expansion of productive forces and differential allocation of profit, were made possible in part by the exercise of bio-power in its many forms and modes of application." Famously, Foucault misplaces and mistimes this observation to Europe's mid-eighteenth century. He does this in part because the great critical archaeologist of man fails, as Wynter teaches us to do, to make the necessary distinction between man and human, so that he can only see a certain "accumulation of men." As a result, for so many contemporary scholars, the mystery, missed in being properly submitted to the understanding, is mistaken for a figure that is hoarded in vaults made of the broken bodies that accrue to mastery. They say, the dead concept, trapped in its own dispersed residue, gives off a kind of light. But black study is already so far in the black that it can only be valued, and therefore (un)read, as a worthless thing – out of time, out of joint, out of here. Its office is impossible and impertinent, which is the condition of all undercommon study today, of all fugitive flesh in communal service.

Black study's chronic making of a living is unpayable debt served without mastery. This unfathomable and incalculable secret, which cannot be enclosed by mastery, is miraculously, wonderfully, *open*. What the book says is what we sing for all to hear. Black study is open access to the inaccessible, which ruptures explanation, which can't help but resist and exceed, always making the surplus that even capital has to live on. Capital, in fine Batailléan fashion, will nonetheless try to calculate, expropriate, and burn this excess. Thus gratuitous financialization, whether imposed on (dead) black bodies or on (failed) black nations, goes on and on until we claim the debt that goes on and on, singing there are no black bodies, there are no black nations. When there is nothing to govern, nothing to secure, there is blackness. We have to come to terms with that. That's what we have to wait on. That's what we have to serve. With this, we are on fire.

He was talking out of the book and we were thinking that this turn from enslavement to religion only gives us, at best, a kind of voluntary service and with that, wouldn't we be in the realm of civil society or freedom of religion? But he was talking out of the book, with her, remotely, and the turn became involuntary, no longer relying on the freedom of the subject, to which the subject is chained. We were thinking, then, that maybe what happens with we who are marked by enslavement and who claim that dispossession, where unpayable debt is unforgivable and forgiven, where the payable debt that can never be paid off is known as liberty, where the debt is black and the indebtedness is blackness, is that we find, in service, that there can be no volunteer. In that happening, we were thinking, the illusion of voluntary service, or attendance, or aid, or being an acolyte, not only cannot stay intact but, in breaking, visits upon its practitioners the most terrible enforcement of the involuntary.

Then they started singing in tongues. The debt of racialization is always all around us and yet, as racialization, can never be summed up, counted, or assimilated to one (number). Greek credit is not Jamaican credit or Puerto Rican credit (just look at the way neither of the latter have been talked about in terms of their Left traditions, though what the International Monetary Fund did to Michael Manley makes Angela Merkel look like a saint). But racialized credit (there's no other kind since capitalism) is a reaction to a particularly disturbing kind of abolition that seeks an old-new debt, that needs mutual aid, that is given to attend, that does not serve society but rather socializes service. The note that can be paid, and must be paid, shadows life, holds it in a tired ravenously mortgaged duet, mistitled life and debt, a phrase whose rhythm misleads, particularly insofar as the death debt signifies turns – by living, in living on, as its mysterious series – on mastery. The dead want to take credit for good debt but the bad debt we owe to living means, not to dead ends, grows in being tended to in service. Baruch Spinoza might say that it is joyous.

Slave, from the Latin *servus*, can't help but give you pause. But that's why service can't be voluntary, why it's always given as disruption of the very idea of the volunteer. Is there a way to think about service in relation not so much to slavery but to fugitivity? You have to remember that slave means fugitive, that essential to the slave, in and as an ensemble of living practices, is fugitivity, which the workshop of Orlando Patterson wouldn't understand. That the condition of the slave forbids voluntarity turns out to be compatible with the fact that the condition of the slave, which is the very idea of the slave's constant undoing, is that the slave is always already fugitive. The slave is constantly escaping being constantly undone. What might it be, then, to be in service, or to be indebted, to this constant escape, which for us takes the form of feel, or manifests itself as feel's constant generation of form in and out of the informal? We serve the general feel, which is as involuntary as breathing, as a syncopated field of heartbeats, in and through a hard and endless row of being beaten.

Incessant collection, unceasing accumulation. Still down on the farm but angled, Angola'd, underneath Tim McGraw's ghastly, unconscious, consciously dronish, delusionally but appropriately good time Louisiana. We constantly pay. Our time is hard and we know that. We feel that. Somehow, something good keeps coming out of that, like a runaway, out of time, out of joint, out of here. The shit is terrible. The good debt, which is constantly paid, which can be paid but never paid off, endlessly accrues and multiplies. This is the hyperfinancialization of living black, capital's irrational, illegitimate, Jeffersonian reproduction. With every new Hemings he gave the lie to his own argument against Alexander Hamilton. The plantation is the First Bank of the United States. The plantation is the Federal Reserve. The good debt that is never paid off is opposed to the bad debt that is never paid, only ever partially remitted and only in name, gesturally, appositionally, tragicomically, in the rich, deadpan austerity of our refusal of austerity. We be barbecuing in the park, roasting these beautiful chestnuts all over the agora.

What if what it is to be European is simply that one occupies the position of creditor in relation to what is imposed upon blackness as the conceptual embodiment of financialization, of endless capitalization? Certain Greeks – Aristotle's true, authoritarian heirs – may want to remain in Europe, as the remains of Europe, as its dregs. After all, Europe's remainder will still have borne the honor of being called Europe's essence, its slave-built treasures liberally sprinkled throughout the museums of all the great capitols. Europe can't leave alone even what it left and leaves behind. Meanwhile, the new metoikic field, the subcitizenry's ineradicable and undocumented trace, is out on the streets all night studying and practicing a new dialectic of wealth and poverty in order to undermine the creditor's monopolization of the capacity to live beyond the means to live. Can we detach what it is to service the debt, or to serve in debt, from the credit economy's brutal requirement to pay on time, in proud time, in (Greenwich) mean time, all the time, in that vulgarity's brutal and supposedly endless 'progression'?

Third Layer

And so, we arrive, borne, again by Carter, at the politico-ecclesiastical performativity of ingestion. This is not a *Meditation on Human Redemption*. Hey Somebody, assuming a body is like exhuming some body, only bloody. Take and eat. This is not my body. The surreal presence is a matter of living in debt.

The fucked-up thing about all the fucked-up things about slavery, the terrible peculiarity of the institution as such, is that it includes – and not as a progressive arc but rather as an aggressively and constantly co-present ensemble – this constant interplay between the animated flesh of the laborer, the conceptual abstraction of and from that flesh into a body with labor power, and the further abstraction from that body into a financial instrument. Slavery had all that going on already, all the time. It is, more precisely and more emphatically, the reduction of body to flesh, as Spillers describes it, *and* the imposition of body and/in its conceptualization upon flesh, as Spillers implies, which comes – by way of some horrible miracle of belatedness – both after and before that reduction. The imposition of body as/in its conceptualization comes before and after flesh *but it never comes first*. The conceptualization of the body is a regulative and regulatory response to flesh, to an exhausted and exhaustive maternal ecology that is submitted to an im/possibility of the mother to which it never submits. The black mother is the very form of black study. Black maternity is black study, as flesh, as force, as feel but not as figure. She is hated because she lives a form of life against all the fucked-up odds of service without master(y). In living black study, as the undercommons of service itself, she is not she, though she bears everything, as a touch between sisters who know what it is to serve, to minister, to cure.

And church is a project, not a place, as Carter whatsays Ruby Sales's singing. Immediately we start to pray on its necessary and righteous displacement. We shall be moved, evidently, as experimental collectivities fray in the interest of our earthly and inconsistent totality. How we can't be stopped is all bound up with the end of everything, towards which policy and improvement hurl us with cold, logistical fury. Our surreption in thrownness is off repeated. Experimental ensembles are ubiquitous in their constant disappearance. As Robin Kelley says, the Civil Rights movement was not a mass movement; it was a whole bunch of little speculative parishes that sometimes coalesced into unbuilt, splay cathedral or, deeper still, in the continuous invention of certain basic anacharismatic, anathematic anthems. It was always way more about Wednesday than it was about Sunday, which is why they send the drones on Wednesday. What if the one we now call intellectual or artist frays in curation, lay ministers unto inadministration, in service in observance of certain lost and found ceremonial) practices (as Wynter sounds, in *Maskerade*, of Jonkunnu), which constitute and generate and preserve (in constant expenditure and differentiation) our insovereign reservoir of social matter and energy?[63] Then that one would be more + less than that, anarchically grounding the difference between rule by obedience and obedience to rule in mutual, under-monastic instrumentality, where we love our flesh like Baby Suggs tells us to. So, you ground with what Karl Marx says the commodity is. You have to grind on that, to see if you can save the commodity (the benefit, the convenience, our differential convening, the modality of our active, differential entanglement) from the hierarchies of exchange that taint it. Those forms are vile because they move within the ascription of value. Is there an invaluable commodity? Yeah.

You can't separate governance from service unless you radically redefine what it is to serve, to care, to curate, to convene.

It's like a ghost be on you, and you're ridden by uprising in near repose, in frenzy's slow drag, along continual lines of misunderstanding – a missing or an avoidance of the understanding in a kind of shelter of waiting on, in a weeping-willow cabin, and you would not understand it. Slowness in acceleration makes you apprehensive, anaperceptive, forgetive, as if you were a bell, an associative velocity of held resonance, the concept's experimental, sentimental sediment. Slow understanding parries (the) understanding's thrust. Recursive water's breakneck deliberation drips corrosive violence to form the recess of what she makes us listen to. What fits in the blank shapes another margin. A modesty, a chastity, of the broken book's broken anglish. Pre-parrying, after-partying, with space still left for strife, in strife's coiled speech, frayed as the sonnet's advent and indenture and Cecilian indentation, a sonata, more and less, to celebrate her feast day, her mass, her public service.

AGAINST MANAGEMENT
Watermelon Mannishness

> The collective working machine… becomes all the more perfect the more the process as a whole becomes a continuous one.
> – Karl Marx

> We decided to shoot it both ways. Except I only shot it my way.
> – Melvin Van Peebles

The Capstone

There was a class called *The Capstone* at Singapore Management University. It was a final, fourth-year course. The students were business students, accounting students, economics students, and a few social science students. The capstone introduced students to thinking in the humanities, somewhat paradoxically, in their final year. The premise was that thinking with these texts would allow students to reflect on their four years at university and think about the paths upon which they were about to embark. The curriculum included figures like Marx, Freud, and Fanon, mixed with more contemporary thinkers and artists like Singapore's Kuo Pao Kun and India's Arundhati Roy. It was all new to the students, but they seemed to enjoy it.

In fact, at the end of the course we'd had such a good time that it was tempting to give all the students marks that reflected their enthusiasm and effort. But the instructor wasn't supposed to do that. They were restricted by a 'suggested' grade distribution that was, really, a compulsory bell curve. So, all they could do was teach the history of the bell curve to these students who were to be submitted to it. In practice, under the imposition of the notorious curve, they could give, at most, thirty-five percent of these students A's. They could try arguing that as fourth-year students the students can be said to have reached a level of competence where more should receive A's, and that these marks would reflect the successful effort over four years to educate them. But that would be missing the point. The students will never be competent. There will always be room for improvement – indeed, for continuous improvement. But that is not quite right either. There are instances where the students are deemed competent. At the moment they are presented to employers they are presented as highly competent. And at the moment they are admitted to the university they are accepted as the best and the brightest. These moments are real. But the moment of grading is equally real. This alternation – between praising and appraising the students – is a continuous one in their university careers. It forms the medium of their daily life at the university. Around them hang posters of SMU students who have achieved everything – images of students who found good jobs with an accounting firm and continued drumming or cycling careers on the side – or of students who swam with dolphins while recreating during their time in coveted internships with financial services. This exaltation of students is a state they are themselves supposed to embrace and embody. Courses on Leadership, on Negotiations, indeed this capstone, are designed to foster this exalted self.

But this is only half of what SMU calls its "value proposition." Students must also submit themselves to constant evaluation of their value. They are to be measured and graded competitively against each other and against their future selves. And as much as they go into this competition with the confidence of being designated as 'the talented tenth' of Singapore, there is inevitably something degrading about the subsequent evaluation, about the assigning of values to each of them, about the valuation they undergo. Their efforts are turned to numbers, the numbers are aggregated and ranked, and as anyone who has ever received a plea for a change of grade knows, a neurotic mix of hubris and shame characterizes the outcome. But it is not really an outcome. It is, indeed, a value proposition. It is a promise of future value, and the value only has value amid the artificial scarcity the bell curve and its meritocratic rule enforce. Moreover, this value proposition remains always unproven, always unfinished, and therefore always an improper, and even indecent, proposition. What is on offer is a student who has been both exalted and degraded, and who is competent, above all, in oscillating between the two. The student is capable of leadership and subservience. The student embodies the business phrase 'USP' – a unique selling proposition. A USP offers the purchaser a chance to buy something unique, just like everyone else. But this hardly unique purchase comes with the ability to revise its price constantly.

Usually, in the capstone, the instructor and the students could get the feeling the class was going well, and that they were creating some novel ways of thinking about the readings and films and their common situation. But when the time for grading comes, the university forces them to individuate that feeling or, really, forces them to individuate that feeling in groups of A students, or B students, or C students. But it isn't just that they are forced to do it. The students want the grades – the good grades – because this valuation stands for a level of access to their more exalted side as it was supposedly displayed in the classroom. Of course, that exalted side is shown only in and as the degraded complement to the grade, the individuated, reduced version of what they'd had together, which is accessed through the desire for access. And it's not that access itself is mere subservience or submission to logistical demands. It involves precisely this bargained oscillation, a willingness to be valued for purposes of devaluation, to be accessed for the promise of a wealth of access. The instruction in creativity and criticality was precisely in the service of this double invitation.

The instructor submits to the university, grading and degrading on the curve, acceding to its claim of access to what goes on underneath it. The students submit to the firm, desiring their (de)gradation into good value propositions, gaining access to it in unequal exchange for the firm's access to their newly acquired creativity and criticality, their newly won competence in leadership and subservience. Whatever had been shared in the classroom makes all this possible. And if it was necessarily deformed in this straightening out for access, that doesn't mean the students – which is all the instructor had found that *they* ever were, and could be – shouldn't try to take it back.

The Algorithm

When the instructor tried to give out too many A's the Dean's Office would write to "request" that the grades be "moderated." But it wasn't actually necessary to do anything in order to fulfill the request. The instructor merely went online and pressed a tab called "moderate grades." An algorithm does the rest. It is not the first time and certainly not the last time that these students will be graded by an algorithm. In grading them and in their acceptance of the grade, the instructor and the students agree to divide up whatever they'd had together in the classroom. They agree to divide and reduce it to all the exhortations to creativity and criticality, and all the efforts at uniqueness and authenticity. The class was individualized, enumerated, dematerialized, and submitted to set's paradoxes. Those with A's will then step forward, exalted while those without A's will be exhorted to step forward, to react by asserting their subjectivity in order to make the next grade. The more they can help individuate the class, the more they can be identified individually with what happened collectively in that class, the better they will be graded. This *subject reaction* is provoked by continuous measurement. This subject reaction is a turn, a recoil. And it is one that has been subject to the speed-up, which occurs when the algorithm is put to work, when logistical capitalism kicks in, when continuous improvement and total quality management trigger this oscillation between praising and appraising, between exaltation and shame. The continuous demand for access, the continuous theft of our means, which is given most emphatically when they are transformed into fantasmatic ends, requires the constant reassertion of our individuality not least because it is this individuality we sell for parts. That is, it is our personality or purported subjectivity we sell to be accessed in as many ways as we can. The subject reaction is the only way to get paid. Classically, the subject reaction's relay between exaltation and shame operates in its confrontation with the fact that the higher truths to which mind aspires must be delivered through the baser faculties of sense. The concept of body is supposed to mediate by organizing sensual experience in units that can be counted, averaged, and sanitized. Some of this classical bourgeois subject reaction may recognizably operate in the instructor and the student, but mostly they are just trying to pull themselves together, to join and differentiate the various swarm of feeling good, in the face and behind the back of logistical demands.

This production of the subject reaction is the dematerialization and individuation of logisticality, *which logistics effects*. Our critical and creative efforts in the classroom, and our grading, are part of this dematerialization, and submit to its logistical demands, not because they do not begin well, but because they do not end well. *They end with degraded means.* Such a dematerialization has deep roots in the Western tradition of positing a subject and its mind. But today it is at work most frenetically and most (in)visibly in logistical capitalism, powered by the algorithm. Logistics today mobilizes and networks us as never before. It asserts us as means as never before. It opens access everywhere and in everything. And, at the same time, logistics degrades those means and denigrates this access by driving them always toward a single end through valuation. That end is surplus: stolen, accumulated, regulated. By tapping our invaluable means to do this, logistics also confronts what we have called our logisticality, our capacity to be a means for itself, in selfless, unplotted, non-local incompleteness. Indeed, we can read the rise of logistics and the subject reaction that it encourages and instructs as attempts to regulate our logisticality. Logisticality is more than a counter-logistics, a countering of logistics. It is our means of movement, and our movement as means. Logistics seeks to impose a position, direction, and flow on our movement, our pedesis, our random walk, our wandering errancy, to trap us in this oscillation, this neurotic pacing back and forth. Logistics wants to position us, to have us take a position, and fortify, and settle. And yet logistics itself also has to keep moving even in its degraded way. This is where the algorithm gets put to work.

Operations management

The capstone students were in the right place to attempt to study this laboring of the algorithm. The class read Marx on alienation, and then read him on the senses too – on how the senses might become theoreticians in their practice. They read Marx talking about nature losing its mere utility by becoming human use, or by fully becoming means. Logistics, however, requires us to utilize our means rather than to (sensually, thoughtfully) practice (as) them. Our senses have long been understood as the means to knowledge, but not often as social means without ends, which is not the same as if they were ends in themselves but is, rather, that they are means in themselveslessness; not as theoreticians in their own right but, rather, in a rite that is not owned but shared in a jurisgenerativity whose making and unmaking is given in a general disbursement way on the other side of right's philosophy. On the one hand, logistics intensifies the opportunities to live a sensuous collective life that is immediately material in its means and as its means. But on the other hand, logistics also wants to dematerialize our means, to abstract them and submit them to the concept – the concept of valuation, and the concept of profit.

And most immediately, logistics wants to submit our means to the concept of flow. The class could well have studied Marx for this insight too. He predicted that "continuous flow" in capitalist production would increasingly become the focus of productivity efforts and would increasingly contribute to profit. But even though the capstone did not study his predictions on flow, Marx has been taken up and dematerialized in the business school by the discipline of operations management. Looking at operations management in a way it would not look at itself, we could say it is a capitalist science that studies the relationship between variable and constant capital *in motion*. Operations management understands itself as the science of the factory, and especially of the assembly line, and even more particularly of what we might call after Marx (and, in a different vein, Raymond Williams), "the flow of the line." By the flow of the line we mean operations management's attention not to workers or machines, nor even to the relationship between the two. While other management sciences, focus on variable capital, like the study of organizational behavior, or on constant capital, like accounting, what characterizes operations management is attention to a certain kind of motion. Not the assembly line then but the assembly line's motion, in flow. Operations management focuses on workers and machines as they appear along the flow of the line in order to *make* that flow line *flow*. In other words, the flow of the line mediates the relationship between worker and machine and determines, rather than is determined by, the proportions of variable and constant capital.

For operations management, the relationship of man to machine means nothing in itself. Managers are indifferent to it. But the relations of man and machine to the flow of the line, and particularly to the motion of that flow, mean everything. In other words, the attention to process, and more recently to the continuous improvement of that process, is the real object of study for operations management. Operations management organizes dead and living labor not just on the flow of the line, but directs it toward the quality of that flow, focusing on its process rather than its product. A machine or a worker is not judged independently but only in service to that flow of the line, in submission to the process. Improvement in quality in operations management is, despite its own rhetoric, not about product but about process. The product – especially that which Marx teaches us is the first product, namely, *the workers*, who will find themselves under subsequent regimes of operations management forced into the same subject reaction that overwhelms and overdetermines the capstone – is really of no interest. With continuous improvement it will be clearer than ever that the worker – like every other commodity, like every other thing – will be dishonored and discarded for the sake of the flow. The commodity, the thing, the worker is neither means nor end. The end is profit and the means are continuous flow. The product, the thing, the speaking commodity, even the power or value or meaning it bears, is nothing but an adjunct to this process.

In its frank indifference to worker, machine, and even product, operations management sets itself apart from the discourses of other business practices. This is not to suggest that operations management is somehow more honest about capitalist work relations, but only that it is a standpoint from which we glimpse a larger indifference that might fuel the fantasy of a world without labor, frictionless and free. By contrast, human resource management or organizational behaviorism must be invested in what would today be called human capital, even if investment is akin to the encouragement we might give our students in the classroom to express themselves – that is, part and parcel of a dematerialization that makes the flow work and the work flow. But even these other disciplines in business bear the mark of this flow. In the discipline of strategy, the leader is exalted, while strategy's other half – decision-making – deploys algorithms that expose the leader as a subject reaction to the flow. Operations management is different only in that it started with no such mediations.

Quality

The emergence of operations management – as with all the disciplines in business – can be traced to class struggle, although the popular story of its rise omits this foundation. According to this popular narrative, recited in textbooks and in the journalism of the business press, the emerging threat of Japanese 'competitiveness' and what would come to be called 'Toyotaism' focused minds in the United States on the importance of quality and consistency in highly durable goods. Implausibly, this rise of 'quality' in Asia is then attributed to American business consultants. This popular story is so preposterous that even business historians, not given to radical dissent, cannot condone it. Yet year after year since 1951, the Deming Prize, which recognizes outstanding contributions to the field of Total Quality Management, continues to be handed out with as little irony as the Nobel Peace Prize and with generally richer rewards. The Deming Prize recognizes individuals or organizations for outstanding efforts in what is today called Total Quality Management, which, when the prize originated, was simply called 'quality.' In fact, the prize's creation was part and parcel of the efforts of imported American business consultants, led by W. Edwards Deming himself, to promote quality control in Japanese businesses after the war. The common narrative begins with American business consultants such as Deming, who were said to have broken through the collectivist culture of Japanese workers at the very moment when post-War American industrial relations were allegedly characterized by a similar collectivism in the legacy of New Deal compromises on collective bargaining and productivity agreements. In the early 1950s, Deming and his colleagues introduced quality management techniques in Japan that aimed to make *individual* workers responsible for the smooth functioning of their part of the assembly line – in other words, for its flow. There were two components of this responsibility. One was reducing mistakes that impacted on the quality of the product. This was to be done by making each worker responsible for those mistakes. The other was improvement, or, speeding up the flow. What quality management sought to do was individualize the speed-up, making it a matter of the worker's personal responsibility. A big part of this was decollectivizing resistance to the speed-up. The result was a worker caught in the oscillation between submitting oneself to the line, to the flow, and asserting one's individuation as a quality controller. The flow continued to be a force well beyond the control of the worker, but rather than responding to it with another collective force, the worker was now individually responsible for his or her response, which was to constitute both submission and optimization.

Despite the pressure Deming and other American overseers placed on Japanese workers in industry, productivity in Japan, contrary to the received storyline, did not improve at all in those years. But if the experiment was a failure as a productivity tool, this is not to say it failed as a management tool deployed amidst the intense labor strikes and worker solidarity that characterized Japan in the 1950s. Meanwhile, the Americans still managing Japan indirectly were already shifting to the tried and true American industrial strategy: government intervention and market distortion. First, they demanded that all their Asian post-War client states, inherited from the British, French, and Dutch, start to give Japanese imports preferential treatment, even at the expense of American products. Then, with the onset of war in Korea, the Americans increasingly put Japanese industry back on a war footing in order to supply their imperial belligerence. As a result, the Japanese economy took off in the direction of its post-War miracle and, with the same distortion later applied by way of the American war on Vietnam, Japan's economy became legend. Deming and company had nothing demonstrable to do with this miracle. But they were in the right place at the right time, when American business needed its own 'productivity solution.'

If the increase in Japanese industrial productivity is essentially fictive, so too is the ascendancy of quality. The oil shocks of 1973 and 1978 – part of a complex class struggle in the oil-producing regions, as the Midnight Notes Collective teach us – coincide not with the more reliable, higher quality Japanese durable goods that are supposed to be the products of a management miracle, but with cheaper cars that have better fuel efficiency. These cheaper cars appear amidst another class struggle not unrelated to the one in the oil fields. It is here that we can pick up the thread of operations management, especially 'quality control,' and its latent power as a class weapon. For while there is no evidence that total quality management was in any way responsible for the Japanese miracle, it was a useful tool in disciplining a collectivist insurgency in Japanese labor. Moreover, in the 1970s with the final breakdown of productivity deals in the United States, amid wildcat strikes and the rise of organizations like the League of Revolutionary Black Workers in Detroit's auto industry, American management was looking for a new form of control. It is here that the failed management theory of Deming and company, burnished by the rise, for very different reasons, of competition in the car, electronics, and machine industries with Japan, finally had its day.

Kaizen in America

Kaizen means 'improvement' in Japanese and Chinese. Used in operations management in Japanese car factories, the term designated not just improvement but continuous, unceasing improvement as the responsibility of each worker on that flow line. With the advent of kaizen 'philosophy' comes the concept of optimizing flow as a mode of worker discipline. Worker discipline will have been optimized precisely because flow cannot be – if the flow of the line will never be good enough workers can constantly be submitted to this deficit, which they embody and internalize in an unceasing mechanics of (e)valuation. As the leading Japanese popularizer of the term in the English-speaking world,

Masaaki Imai, puts it, "kaizen means continuous improvement by everyone, everyday, everywhere." The rise of kaizen means there will no longer be the pursuit of Frederick Taylor's "one best way." Measurement – which had reassured us that we had found that best way and completed the job – would be replaced by metrics, powered by the algorithm. With kaizen we could say valuation shifted from the product to the process. A product has a value that can be measured in a price-making market. A process has a value that can only be temporarily read. The value of process is contingent, thereby rendering value a process in itself. This is why a financial product would be more accurately called a financial process – its value rests on ongoing metrics, or perhaps we should say its value never rests because of ongoing metrics, because of the ongoing improvement and acceleration of metrics. Metrics, here, is a kind of post-classical mechanics, whose detachment from any fundamental questions concerning *nature of value* make it a mindlessly powerful instrument for classical political economy and its underlying metaphysics of value. This quantum metrics is also based, in part, on an uncertainty principle, whose name is efficiency. Nothing can be deemed efficient without giving rise to the question of its efficiency. Operations management turns its attention away from efficiency measured by the profit realized by the commodity, and toward efficiency of the process, efficiency as the process, which is measured only momentarily. Continuous improvement means that every efficiency became inefficient the moment it is measured. Gradually, measurement itself becomes inefficient and is replaced by metrics, the relative taking of a measure that 'benchmarks' the flow in order to speculate on it, using the algorithm. The goal is for the flow line to outperform itself; or, in other words, with kaizen the goal is given as and shifts with speculation on the flow, itself, and not its productivity.

Of course, there has long been a drive in capitalist firms for relative surplus, and even longer has there been pressure for efficiencies through capitalist competition. But with kaizen, attention to the flow of the line for its own sake becomes paramount and efficiency is detached from anything like measurable competition or market mechanisms. Continuous improvement makes speculative finance possible. Kaizen not only predated contemporary speculative finance's entrance into the factory gates but also, crucially, served to link speculative finance to (the classical mechanics of) assembly line productivity. Now, the flow of the line itself represented potential. The assembly line became speculative or, rather, its flow did. Accounting shifts to include metrics for this speculative line, and finance moves in, in force. Everything is sold off (and rented back) except the speculation of the flow. Firms (and later even banks) are hollowed out in this process but not emptied. This is not a matter, as is sometimes portrayed, of firms becoming victims of financialization. On the contrary, kaizen makes financial speculation possible. What remains in the firm after financialization is speculation on the flow. The terms used for this speculation on the flow of the line are 'core competencies,' or sometimes the infamous 'competitive advantage,' and, today, 'value proposition.' All of these management concepts emerged to signal that a firm's management team has a method for improving the flow of the assembly line, in any kind of assembly, to get more value out of workers by intensifying access to them. The reason to invest in newly evolving 'resource-based' firms is not because they hold certain assets, or make certain commodities, but because they and their management demonstrate the capacity continuously to improve the flow of a line through deeper access to workers, whether through technology or workplace cultures that extend their reach into every area of workers' lives. The means of production itself thereby enters the speculative realm with kaizen. Today, this logic culminates in private equity firms who, with complete indifference, buy, disassemble, and reassemble not businesses but *business processes*, or so they say.

Quality and Brutality

This is half of the picture. Because, of course, improvement has always been speculative, and speculation, despite today's rhetoric, has always, however surreptitiously, been about the possibilities of cheapening labor or speeding up the machines, whether it was the farmer's capacity to improve land, or the enslaved woman's capacity to exceed her insurance. It is in this context that we speak of usufruct as the coming together of two kinds of improvement – the improvement of self and the improvement of property in the eighteenth and early nineteenth century. When Hegel speaks of usufruct in the *Philosophy of Right* as the placing of two wills in one property, he has just completed a discussion of slavery; so that while he discusses usufruct without mentioning human property, it is impossible not to read this passage not only as essential to his understanding of the essential relation of law to the modern state but also as emanating from an equally essential relation of the problem of improvement to the dialectic of master and slave, which structures and conditions the *Phenomenology of Mind*. Neither modern philosophy nor the modern subject nor the modern state can be free of this interplay of bondage and improvement. Usufruct is not just the working of another's land, but of an other, in and for a self that is thereby worked and worked on; and the wills that clash in the matter of improvement are propelled by racial and sexual capitalist accumulation and demonstrations of self-issuing will, bound together. Usufruct therefore entails not just the insertion of the self-improving will into the thing but also the violative assertion of a necessarily etiolated will as intrinsic to that thing. In this regard, a man can be turned into a thing only insofar as he is first a man. The slave's humanity is not just necessarily violated; it is also, quite simply, necessary, as Hartman teaches us. Dehumanization follows humanization, and does not simply negate humanity in the flow of brutality that sweeps man to his politico-economic destiny.

Usufruct was itself never going finally to be done and there was always another property or body into which one needed to place a putatively independent self-improving will, in order to improve that thing. This speculation on the line resulting from kaizen – the brutal decollectivization and individuation of the line that is at the same time a sociopathological demand for access to the individuated worker – has its origins in the slave labor farms producing cotton in the United States, and sugar in the West Indies and South America, as the black history of slavery clearly shows. Slave work gangs are spread along a line of cotton plants, or sugar cane, and forced to improve continuously; and any cooperation amongst them is brutally punished, punished more severely even than the failure to improve, precisely because it disrupts the simple, individuative arithmetic that undergirds even the most mathematically exotic and sophisticated metrics. In the fields, there was no question of a subject reaction not least because it was refused by the enslaved without ever having been offered. Indeed, those who claim nothingness as opposed to those who make much ado about willfulness would eventually be forced toward burdened individuality. But the brutal irony remains that the subject reaction, the hard-won access to being accessed when liberation takes a liberal term, disavows the openness management and administration steals and fills at our peril. That openness, that nothingness, that vulnerability, that affectability, that inaccessible accessibility that we share, is all we have.

Logistics

The imperium of cotton and sugar not only hosted these fiendish early experiments in breaking collectivity on the line and inserting and asserting wills but also gave us an early glimpse of an integrated global supply chain. The breeding and marching or shipping of the enslaved southward and westward from Tidewater and Piedmont plantations, or inland from the Caribbean and Pacific Coasts of Colombia, to make crops financed through speculation on their torture-enforced, metric-imposed labor; and the bales of cotton or barrels of molasses loaded on ships in New Orleans or Bridgetown, insured in London, bound for Liverpool's wholesale clearinghouses or Massachusetts distilleries, are links in a global value chain created by bankers, planters and slavers. But it is only in our time that this supply chain becomes fully integrated with the flow of the line *inside* the factory gates. Around the same time that operations management was coming to understand kaizen and the valuation of the flow of the line itself, it was also rethinking the linearity and finitude of the line. It is at this point that a new subdiscipline in operations management becomes firmly established as a rigorous academic discipline in the business schools: logistics. Of course, logistics already existed as a practice going back in military affairs as long as there have been sieges, invasions, and forts. Food, water, weapons, and people had to be transported and maintained to support any strategy of war. The African and Trans-Atlantic slave trade represented the great, hideous introduction of mass logistics for commercial rather than military or state purposes. It became the ghoulish lab of experiment in access for singular means of work and sex, worldmaking and subjectivization. Much would follow, including infrastructure projects for the circulation of people, goods, and information and, of course, more mass displacements, indentures and migrations in the brutal enforcement against indigenous peoples and he very idea and practice of indigeneity of the law of genocide and geocide. All of this logistics would not only bear this trademark of 'continent of origin' in the slave trade, but with usufruct the improvement of flow would become indistinguishable from racialization. Whiteness, as racialization's origin and residuum, where access is imposition and submission in self-protection and self-determination rather than practicing incompleteness, is the self-improvement of flow. Blackness becomes what it already was, the prior interruption, the sabotage to come, the incapacity to breathe into the flow as the capacity for breath as means, for the breadth of means.

It is little wonder, then, that when the modern idea of the economy appears, as Timothy Mitchell teaches us, the discipline emerges shackled to racial science. Mitchell reminds us that the founding American economist, the one who inaugurates the discipline by building the first working model of this independent 'economy,' was not incidentally a racist and eugenicist, but necessarily so. Irving Fisher theorized that economics should be the study of money and what today would be called human capital. Both, according to Fisher, could be improved (and therefore speculated upon). But "racial degeneracy" meant that some had no understanding of the future. The degenerate races had therefore no desire or ability to improve. They would have to have their utility maximized for them, by usufruction.

Logistical Capitalism

By the time operations management joins economics as a science of improvement and speculation, containerization and extended value chains of global production and markets turn study of this flow into a core obsession with who and what generated or degenerated. As a result, operations management comes to see that which was moving *in and out* of the factory as extensions of the flow of the line *inside* the factory. Paying attention to these extensions can improve the flow inside that factory. Logistics, reverse logistics, user communities, and relationship marketing are now seen as part of a continuous process that can be continuously improved before inputs enter the factory, while they are transformed in the factory, and after outputs leave the factory. These extensions serve to improve the process by taking into account the way the movement and condition of raw materials, or customer use, reinvention, and feedback can lead to further continuous improvement of the line. In other words, operations management sees itself as responsible for all the circuits of capital and not just production. The flow pours out of the factory door and floods the world, submerging its political bodies.

This forward and backward integration and management of the value chain was accomplished through metrics and the algorithm. Logistics has long been a field for algorithmic experiment centered on the 'traveling salesman problem,' which is concerned with determining the most efficient route, and the 'Canadian traveler problem,' which is concerned with finding the most efficient adaptations en route. What logistical theorists sought from the algorithm was continuous recalculation – metrics not measurement. The evolution of the algorithm in logistics tends towards the elimination of "the controlling agent" – living labor – and with that the elimination of "human time," as the logistics literature likes to call it. In the fantasies of logistics theory, intimated in the discourse of the 'internet of things,' where a general dehumanization – which humanization anticipates – is imagined, things will have developed a kind of plasticity in response to changes in the environment, transforming themselves without the intervention of living labor. Both the material developments of logistics and the immaterial interventions of logistics theory have consequences for more or less conscious developments in philosophy and science whose conditions of possibility are framed by the methodical algorithm at work and the methodological work of the algorithm in thought.

By the 1980s – as logistics and the performance metric extended and dispersed the interests of the factory, connecting the flow of its production line past the blurred boundaries of input and output – operations management had 'left the factory' and taken kaizen with it. More importantly, operations management and logistics helped business to see how the line could overflow or flow everywhere. In defiance of the regulation and containment that strict linearity implies, the assembly line has not disappeared but become ubiquitous. Today, it is a flow plane, a flood plain, an uncharted dispersal of sovereign impositions with their attendant and incidental subject reactions. General and incalculable communicability is virtualized as total communication, total connectivity. This is capital's algorithmic attempt to dematerialize, conceptualize and regulate an essential and essentially sensual communism; this is capital's determination to gain total access to the means to live beyond means. At stake is that double operation of the degradation of means that the algorithm seeks and seeks to regulate.

Synaptic Labor

Taken together as contemporary phenomena and in their long, braided historical trajectories, these two shifts in operations management – kaizen and logistics – lead us to a different understanding of what is extracted from labor today. Rather than displaying individual labor power, workers must manifest synaptic labor, a capacity for composition given in having been entered, as it were, into the flow of assembly upon command. And with every email, with every text or post, the command is given. One is, at once, instantiated and called upon as data and as syntactic unit. This is logistical capitalism, where what is valued is work directed toward the improvement of the flow, which flows everywhere and over everybody. Workers – if that is the right term for those who are called upon to assemble or asked to operationalize these non-linear, infinite lines of assembly – must connect the flow while also improving it, pass on the data while also enhancing and augmenting and embodying it, enter a given affective zone while providing passage to a new zone, read what is sent while also commenting on what they send. The language of operations management is the language of synaptic labor at work. The terms of operations management have become the terms of our common sense: lead time, flexibility, availability, resources, scheduling, and resource allocation. Synaptic labor plugs in anywhere, translates anything, and one must devise one's own forms of "queue theory" for the flow of lines that run in every direction, like a sea. Workers themselves are responsible for the forms of conditioning that render and maintain their accountability. The importance of the commodity pales in comparison to that of the quality of the flow along which it travels, which is the infrastructure workers make and make better, more resilient.

What is produced is a line whose dispersal as flow is also its narrowing and incarceration, while metrical fantasies of the flow's continual improvement are imposed in a general demand that chokes, constrains, and individuates speculation. In moments of such policed asphyxiation, workers risk becoming what labor never was before: submissive and inanimate. Indeed, individuated subject formation and identity construction *are* this speculative submission, in which the individual subject tends towards his own disappearance in a heroism that can only serve the network. Such speculation inevitably leads to the ultimate fantasy: what if workers could create the (over)flow of a line that does not need them? What if we could create a self-improving flow? This would be tantamount to a self-valorizing capitalism, one that succeeds in its suicidal and murderous drive to be free of labor. The speculative flow, unravelling and joining more and more of us in its rhythm of continuous improvement, drives us to this fantasy, which we perform – or more precisely – out-perform in social death.

Disruptive innovation is the term in management science – especially in the field of strategy – that is used to designate a kaizen event in the social field. A kaizen event is an unexpected turn in the flow of the line, or a surprising insight about that flow, that is then integrated as an improvement to the flow. As Marina Vishmidt astutely points out in the context of contemporary art, this disruption of the flow lines of assembly makes no distinction between the flow and those who reproduce it.[64] We are called things and are then called upon to be nimble Canadian salesmen full of innovative volition in a Great White North gone global. We are everywhere degraded in common loneliness and flattered every day in being made to make new theories of connection. Social life is subject to metrics that seek out and valorize disruption as improvement and improvement as the only metric, leaving any repose in social life – what we would call, with Valentina Desideri, our militant conservation, the fermentation of our desires – subject to attack as anti-social. And so, we must dissemble in order to renew our habits of assembly so we can breathe in the breadth of our means. Communal sensual life emerges in the hapticality of those called upon to assemble this flow, those who dissemble this flow in their renewed assembly, running underground and overhead and undercommon. This is the uncontrollable improvisational effect of a general and material communicability that refuses the virtualization that forms its shadowed, accidental fellow travelers. This living, poetic communicability lays down other lines that it exceeds, riding the blinds, jaywalking the streets, or staying home in sub-domestic, ante-logistic transmutation.

Blackness and the Bug

Subject-reactive recoil can never produce the full refusal, sabotage, or indirection that (the demise of) logistical capitalism requires. Though it is a reaction to the degradation of means, it is itself, in its individuation, a degraded reaction. What synaptic labor does begin to make clear is that any kind of subject formation, or individual identity dematerialized from the general and generative ecology of the society of labor under logistical capitalism, is already bound up with a value chain of brain, mind, identity, and subject. Consider, for instance, as the very embodiment of the very idea of the considered instance, Gregor Samsa, a traveling salesman who wakes up one morning and finds – his body having been accessed so completely by the flow that he cannot move in it, or pass as its embodiment, or accept its passage through him, or foster its improvement – that he is a bug. He is, in this regard, the apotheosis of individual resistance in individual defeat. He cannot accede to the monstrousness of his body's loss, though this would be the only way for him to block this access, to find a way out or a way off schedule, to keep from being straightened out by another in the flow. His hardness means he can only move wrongly for his family, scurrying, dragging the monstrosity that is his but that he cannot own or control. And rather than being protected by this hardness, this unstraightened movement, his only idea, and that of his family, is that the monstrosity that is not him, or his, must be dematerialized. Gregor the subject must return, to travel and sell, or die. Now, consider the all-but-inconsiderable Jeff Gerber, an insurance salesman who races the bus, in a self-directed act of route efficiency, through his white suburban neighborhood on his way to work. One day, this racist white boy wakes up black. He wakes up black and loses everything and stays alive and makes a claim (on the blues, and the Panthers). He dissembles and, in neither going with the flow nor resisting it alone in a performance of brittle, individual dignity, he looks for his folks, renews assembly, and joins black social life. It's not that he was passing, or that he was passing more than any other white insurance salesman passes, it's just that an eternity of passage – whose overdubbed roar kinda sounds like *¡No pasarán!* – erupted through his false choices and brutal prejudices, overrunning the single track of his simple, single mind.

When we read Franz Kafka with our students we're always asking after Melvin Van Peebles. Instead of urging criticality and creativity to fashion a

knowledgeable self in the wake of catastrophe, we try to see that what kills Gregor is brutal access and its insertions and assertions, not the denial of it that is given in soft flesh, hard shell, and irregular movement, all of which instantiate what Spillers calls a terrible, claimed, empathic availability. What keeps Jeff alive is that he does not turn back but scurries away towards a party for absolutely necessary self-defense, his blackness – which is not his, but which he claims – being precisely the ante-ontic, underontological opacity that logistical capitalism can't pass through and can't let pass.

Our students have to pass, and must be passed. And it makes us think there must be something more than passing. To think of passing suggests that logistics, logistical capitalism, is constantly trying to straighten us out so we will pass, and so it can pass through, which may amount to the same thing. We have to do something for logistical capitalism all the time. We have to act for it, and through it; to keep passing precisely because monstrosity is prior, and logistics is always trying to keep us in this oscillation of straightening and turning back, in reactive counter-subjectivity, (in)to the subjects we're supposed to be, rather than moving on and in this general swerve of sensual incoherence, the mode of study in which self-knowledge is disowned. Logistics knows that to straighten a turn is not to eliminate it but to hold it in a metric, to put it on a schedule of endless optimization, as nervous movement back and forth in a scalar segment, so that it turns on or against the anarchy of turning, thereby rendering itself valuable. Logistics is straight in that metrically degrading way. This is its murderousness, its refusal to attend to contour, its supervisory neglect and, also, its wastefulness, its continual missing of all in its inveterate grasping of everything.

How can we make a monstrous distortion, a spreading bullwhip through the flow? How can hapticality step out on criticality, that brutal, Delphic-oracular imperative to 'know thyself'? How can we join and intensify a general strike against calculation, against valuation? Such a strike wouldn't be an event so much as the emergence of a general condition of exhaustion and radically impure generativity. It would be a crooked blow, with a curved and curling stick picked up on the run in afformative, depositional black repose. How can our study live in the flesh as a refusal (out) of mind, in the break of the flow? Let's re-route Kafka through a passage in Spillers and see if we can refuse to adapt.

The Traveling Salesman's Unclaimed Monstrosity

This passage is our path, our guide, and our propulsion:

> Therefore, the female, in this order of things, breaks in upon the imagination with a forcefulness that marks both a denial and an "illegitimacy." Because of this peculiar American denial, the black American male embodies the only American community of males which has had the specific occasion to learn who the female is within itself, the infant child who bears the life against

the could-be fateful gamble, against the odds of pulverization and murder, including her own. It is the heritage of the mother that the African-American male must regain as an aspect of his own person hood – the power of "yes" to the "female" within.

This different cultural text actually reconfigures, in historically ordained discourse, certain representational potentialities for African-Americans: 1) motherhood as female bloodrite is outraged, is denied, at the very same time that it becomes the founding term of a human and social enactment; 2) a dual fatherhood is set in motion, comprised of the African father's banished name and body and the captor father's mocking presence. In this play of paradox, only the female stands in the flesh, both mother and mother-dispossessed. This problematizing of gender places her, in my view, out of the traditional symbolics of female gender, and it is our task to make a place for this different social subject. In doing so, we are less interested in joining the ranks of gendered femaleness than gaining the insurgent ground as female social subject. Actually claiming the monstrosity (of a female with the potential to 'name'), which her culture imposes in blindness, "Sapphire" might rewrite after all a radically different text for a female empowerment.[65]

And this note from our attorney, Oscar Zeta Acosta, is our (way) station (of the cross).

Somebody still has to answer for all the smothered lives of all the fighters who have been forced to carry on, chained to a war for Freedom just like a slave is chained to his master. Somebody still has to pay for the fact that I've got to leave friends to stay whole and human, to survive intact, to carry on the species and my own Buffalo run as long as I can.[66]

Now, we can read (with) some excerpts from Kafka's letters to his fiancé, Felice Bauer:

I'll write you again today, even though I still have to run around a lot and shall write down a short story that occurred to me during my misery in bed and oppresses me with inmost intensity.[67]

But my story's hero has also had a very bad time today, and yet it is only the last lap of his misfortune, which is now becoming permanent (58).

But don't be unhappy about it, for who knows, the more I write and the more I liberate myself, the cleaner and the worthier of you I may become, but no doubt there is a great deal more of me to be got rid of, and the nights can never be long enough for this business which, incidentally, is highly voluptuous (58).

My little story would certainly have been finished tomorrow, but now I have to leave at 6 tomorrow evening; I get to Reichenberg at 10, and go on to Kratzau at 7 the next morning to appear in court (61-62).

The letters were written in November 1912, as Kafka was writing *The Metamorphosis*, a process/product (trial/sentence) that, a decade later, he would describe as an indiscretion. Kafka's deeply concerned with the logistics of writing, with the proper mode of delivery, but also with the appropriate timetable of construction or composition. *The Metamorphosis* would have been better written, he says, without the interruptions, the stops and starts. If only the line could have been more direct. Everything is filtered through the anxieties that attend the imperative to improve, to optimize. The story of a traveling salesman's problems turns out to emerge from and as a variation on the Traveling Salesman Problem, about which more in exactly one minute. Inefficiency leaves a permanent residue, a taint, a voluptuousness, which simultaneously marks decay and incompleteness and a radical extracompleteness, a metastatic or ante-static monstrosity, an Octavia Butlerian flaw that is also an indescribable sweetness, a Judith Butlerian vulnerability that is also an immeasurable force. We feel compelled to say that Kafka cannot claim this monstrosity but we want to say, also, that his work makes it possible for monstrosity to makes its claim upon us.

At the intersection of modes of inquiry that include theoretical computer science, the theory of computational complexity, and combinatorial optimization there lies something called the Traveling Salesman Problem. The problem is: given a list of cities and the distances between each pair of cities, what is the shortest possible route that visits each city exactly once and returns to the origin city? This problem was given its first mathematical formulation in the mid-nineteenth century by Irish mathematician W. R. Hamilton and was refined in the 1930s and popularized within the fields just mentioned in the 1950s and 1960s. It continues to be a hot topic in mathematics and the natural sciences today, but before its mathematical formulation and formalization it was a problem for business men, stated for and by business men, within the context of a certain set of narratives of *bildung* – of evaluative self-picturing and improvement given in and as a kind of capacity for framing, at the intersection of crafting and imagining. This is, it turns out, where optimization and speciation, management and racialization, converge and this convergence is presented to us as early as 1832 in a book entitled *Der Handlungsreisende – wie er sein soll und was er zu tun hat, um Aufträge zu erhalten und eines glücklichen Erfolgs in seinen Geschäften gewiß zu sein – von einem alten Commis-Voyageur* (The traveling salesman – how he must be and what he should do in order to get commissions and be sure of a happy success in his business – by an old Commercial Traveler). Self-improvement, self-optimization, implies a story, one in which the ladder of success is also always the ladder of misfortune. Gregor's ascent and descent are inseparable from one another and from Kafka's, in the movement within his writing from his stories to their story. In any case, in offering a modest supplement to Jorge Luis Borges's list of Kafka's precursors, we want to argue that *The Metamorphosis* is Kafka's formalization of the Traveling Salesman Problem, which emerges in an investigation of profound, existential homelessness. Because you can't get home once you embark on the business trip whose purpose is to secure one's home. There is no proper return because home isn't there and because, in any case, the one who leaves is never the one who returns and because, deeper still, the one who leaves was never one in the first place. One does not return; one can only turn (in)to one's monstrosity, in the midst of its being constantly turned against, that constant turning against monstrosity being the technical definition of what it is that the

word 'home' designates. The traveling salesman's problem is that he can't make it home. One way to describe *The Metamorphosis* is that it presents us with the necessity and impossibility of claiming homelessness, that monstrosity. It is an indiscretion that discloses the general indiscretion against which improvement violently, brutally founders.

Another way to put it is that monstrosity is improvement gone awry not from but rather before the very beginning. What if the very idea of ownership over one's body is imposed, along with the very idea of one's body, and then immediately taken away by the one who will improve it, put it to better use, and therein establish an indisputable proprietary claim? Ownership can only be proved, can only be demonstrated, in such transfer, wherein the owned is established as monster, as the (failed) embodiment of monstrous disestablishment. Having been improved in having been degraded, their subordinate being, given in and as speciation, constitutes proof of the very idea of ownership. A monstrosity that is given as a more or less uncontrollable generativity, as a profound danger, a metamorphic problem, always unfinished, always in decay, never complete, always simultaneously more and less than one, can only ever be (dis)owned. But is this condition – which at first seems to accrue to having been at once made and undone, something to which we can aspire precisely insofar as it is already in us – held imprecisely in the place where purification is touched by degradation? Kafka wants to be pure and he wants to be free but to arrive at this condition must suffer the fits and starts of writing – of, more precisely, a writing that is concerned with fits and starts, with detours and delays, a writing that is not so much without terminus but, rather, brutally held within an infinite, infinitely subdivided, but bounded terminal. Is there any way that an endless writing – that is, at the same time, a closed writing – can find and claim an opening, which would of necessity be a wounding? We think this is the question Deleuze and Félix Guattari were asking by way of the concept of the minor, or, more precisely, by way of the activity or force (Kafka ambivalently called it the voluptuousness) of minoritization which might be considered in its continuity with monstration and speciation. Think of it as having an apple embedded in your back. It is as if one has not only become more and less than one, but also that here, where decay and generation combine, one has become soil.[68] Within this indiscretion, we have an emblem that intimates the general indiscretion. How can optimization be achieved by way of representations of the non-optimal that are themselves produced under profoundly non-optimal conditions by way of deeply non-optimal methods? And there's a flipside: how can radical resistance to optimization be modeled, as it were, by the ones whose monstrosity is given in their having been most emphatically and profoundly made subject to optimization? More precisely, monstrosity, here, accrues to she whose refusal of the optimization to which she has been submitted is the very condition of her existence. Such monstrosity would be the best of all possible worldlessnesses.

So, what might happen if we think about Gregor's monstrosity, the monstrosity given in the problem of the traveling salesman, the specific homelessness, as the particular impossible domesticity given in and as black female flesh? Spillers discusses the necessity, whose violence is more + less than divine, of claiming the monstrosity that attends what she calls the theft or loss of body, of the capacity or right to, as Salamon puts it, assume a body, while Acosta attends to the insurgent social life that is given in something like a common refusal to (attempt to) compensate for that condition, which, by way of that refusal, must be conceived of as loss *and* finding *and* revolt. The main question we have been driven by is: what if Gregor weren't, because he couldn't be, as a function of his monstrosity, (the only) one? What if, instead of refusing to be a cockroach, he refused to be a cockroach without a people? This is not a question concerning identification via metaphor: like, what if there are others who, via speciation, have lost the capacity to have a body? The question is, rather, what if there is a common social life given in a diverse modality of claims made on monstrosity, in and as shared remonstrance, in a practical demonstration of that which passeth show and, for that matter, individual interiority, too? This would require a new understanding of monstrosity's origins and precipitating conditions. What if Gregor's perversion or perversity were not only not solitary but also not his own? What if it were somehow protruding from the closed system given in the relation between optimization and ownership or, more precisely, what if it were a kind of rustle under a sheet covering a settee, an intimation of an indigent kind of indigeneity, an anindigenous monstrosity that precedes its production-in-improvement, an incessantly demonstrative blackness that can no more be improved upon than proved. At stake, here, is a question concerning the general incompleteness of process, which is different than a fully conceived notion of process that is meant somehow to stand in for and displace incompletion by merely opposing it to product. This concerns a radicalization of process, an activation of its capacity to avoid management. Perhaps, here, we can imagine metamorphosis in its difference from, or as this radicalization of, process; we can think, in other words, *Verwandlung's* resistance to *Verwaltung*. This concerns not only the aggressive officiousness of Gregor's manager but also the ubiquity of management in his life, which leaves it unhoused and, eventually, unlivable. Within this regime, the hopefully liberatory valorization in which process is made to stand against and over product is unavailable. Again, a product has a value that can be measured. A process has a value that can only be temporarily read. It needs a metric to track it, which is to say to hold it in a deadly coupling with product within a commercial metaphysics of productivity. Operations management, whose early manifestation Gregor suffers, turns its attention not to efficiency measured by the profit realized in the commodity but rather to efficiency of the process, measured momently but constantly in the forward and backward integration and management of the value chains that are accomplished through metrics, algorithmically; again, what logistical theorists sought from the algorithm was continuous recalculation, metrics not measurement; and, again, in the genetic and evolutionary generation of algorithms they believe they may have finally eliminated what they call 'the controlling agent' – living labor – and, moreover, 'human error,' as well. This elimination of errancy has a long history, as long as the positing of man in his perfection and the improvement of those who are not but nothing other than man in their degradation, which is both assumed and imposed.

This capacity to think and represent the inability to stave off errancy in the human, to regulate and manage black and inhuman flaw, is what makes us want to think Van Peebles and his ante-hero Jeff Gerber as a precursor to the Kafka we propose, who offers us a picture of Gregor's anti-heroic condition as, in part, an inability to claim a certain monstrosity, an accession rather than a resistance to or refusal of total access. Is there a difference between Gregor and that sassy, all but sapphirically watermelon mannishness – in which one wakes up and realizes that he is not insofar as he is black, which blackness he has been trying to allay in a strenuous regime of constant improvement, so that Gerber is revealed as someone who's been passing all along? Watermelon Man, whose self-improvement breaks down seemingly under its own weight, as if he literally sweated away his own makeup, his own capacity to keep (self-)making up for something, given in and as a whiteface that practically teases us with its audacious visual failure, doesn't die alone in the room that is no longer, but has also never been, his own; rather, he enters into black sociality, walking into the blues with a drink in his hand. In *The Metamorphosis* we propose, Gregor will have realized he was a monster all along thereby claiming, which is to say radicalizing, the status of the shipped, the sold, in a general refusal and suspension of, a general strike against, calculation. The brain, in/and its synapses, is just another bad concept, a brutal conceptualization – by way of body, its spatiotemporal constitution, and its attendant metaphysics of the possessive individual self in networked relationality – of held flesh. What is valued is work directed toward the improvement of the flow, and in the social factory the flow of the line can run anywhere, and we must enter its streams.

But what is the historical economy by which blackness becomes the black and the black becomes a sign (a monster, a demonstration, a showing) of blackness, where blackness derives its name from its sign, from that by which it is announced? The sign works its terrible magic precisely from within a radical non-isolation. It's not just that it signifies an unruly sociality; it actually instantiates and materializes that sociality. The ungovernability of Gregor's limbs, as if he is gifted with the stigmatic charismata of a multi-linear, polyrhythmically funky drummer's independence, is how flesh demonstrates the body's non-assumption, its haptic wakefulness in groundedness, even as it also indicates the agitation that attends having been reduced to atmospheric flow's hub, or nub, in the constant attempt to regulate and vilify affective rub. In the room that is not now nor ever was his own, this interplay of access and ungovernability indicates that Gregor is not in the world. And the way this metoikic staying outside and unhoused at home occurs makes you wonder if he'd ever been in the world and makes you wonder about how it is or what it means to be in the world, to be involved in worldliness as optimization, as this constant necessity of and for improvement. Does Gregor become what improvement forces him to become or does he revert to what improvement was sent to improve? This concerns the relation – between administration and metamorphosis, where improvement is mobilized both to induce and to suppress change – we have to want not to be not able to refuse. Can we embrace such imperfection and keep on imperfecting every old and new logistical collapse? Can we extend and improvise upon the radically generative and degenerative inefficiency of Kafka's writing? Van Peebles teaches us that such failure, such continual detonation of the capstone, is always worth a try.

BASE FAITH

THE EARTH MOVES AGAINST THE WORLD. AND TODAY THE RESPONSE OF THE world is clear. The world answers in fire and flood. The more the earth churns the more vicious the world's response. But the earth still moves; Tonika Sealy Thompson might call it a procession. The earth's procession is not on the world's calendar. It is not a parade on a parade ground. It is not in the world's teleology. Nor is the procession exactly a carnival played to mock or overturn this parade, to take over its grounds. A procession moves unmoved by the world. The earth's procession around which all processions move struts in the blackness of time. And the earthen who move around, and move in earth's procession, move, as Thompson says, like the Sisters of the Good Death in Bahia move, in their own time out of time. God is so powerful in this procession that he cannot exist. Not because he is everywhere in the procession but because we are. We are the moving, blackened, blackening earth. We turn each other over, dig each other up, float each other off, sink down with each other, and fall for each other. We move in earthen procession swaying to base even as its beat alerts the world's first responders. These responders are called strategists. Strategy responds to the constant eruption of the earth into and out of the world. The response takes the form of a concept upon which form has been imposed, which is then imposed upon the earthen informality of life.

Some say it was Alfred Sohn-Rethel who first figured out how the concept was, in this interplay of formation and enforcement, stolen into ownership, abducted and abstracted, weaponized in strategy. He said the abstraction of exchange, and later the abstraction of money, led us to think in the suspension of time and space, the suspension of materiality, and this led to the propriation of the concept. But Sohn-Rethel only picks up the trail of this theft with the thief, the individual, already formed and ready for the strategized and immaterial concept, already formed and readied by it. He wants to convict this thief. We want to take him home.

We want to take him out 'cause out is home. We're at home in the prophetic churning of the earth on the move, the round run of the fugitive, visitation in our eyes, refuge on our tongues. Our unholy commune with those who keep moving and stay there, who keep out before they can be kept out. That's why the hell hounds of strategy are on our trail. They think they got the scent of our leader. But our leader is not one. Let's call her Ali, after Pasolini's Profezia. Ali Blues Eyes. Pasolini thought she was coming in the procession from Africa to teach Paris how to love, to teach London brotherhood, to march east with the red banners of Trotsky in the wind. But she never arrived because we went to chant in Palermo, fast in Alabama, meditate in Oaxaca. So Ali became Tan Malaka and we went to the fête, the jam, the study group.

Ever since capital witnessed Lenin doing it better, capital has been running from strategy. Today when capital deploys a concept everybody is supposed to buy it but no one is supposed to believe it. Capital might call this strategic universality. Or it might not call it anything because capital is not concerned with the dignity or the sovereignty of the concept. The concept served its purpose. And its main purpose now is to get out of the way of logistics or to become logistics' conduit. Its propriety and its proprietary commitments prepare it to be bought and sold into a roughened, airy thinness. Today's concepts in circulation are not the abstraction of or from the commodity; they are commodities and cannot, in their propriety and proprietary form, be used against the commodity-form. Their form is the air the commodity expels, containerized, as all but impalpable units of exhaust(ion). They are just another strategy. And strategy, though it is not abstract, does not really matter, either. What matters is logistics. Logistics, not strategy, provides the imperative. Strategy just provides the friction. Logistics moves the concept around in the circuits of capital. The world's only argument against the earth is logistical. It must be done. The earth's movement must be stopped, or contained, or weakened, or accessed. The earthen must become clear and transparent, responsible and productive, unified in separation. This is not a matter of deploying the concept, strategically or otherwise, but of force, forced compliance, forced communication, forced convertibility, forced translation, forced access. Capital does not argue, though many argue with it.

Capital just likes disruption. Capital's been running from strategy, running toward logistics, running as logistics, running into the arms of the algorithm, its false lover who is true to it. All that's left of strategy is leadership, the command you find yourself in after logistics takes over, when the unit comes into its own. For capital strategy is a just a form of nostalgia, or proof that it has nothing to fear from its enemies who embrace it, proof that they are not enemies. They are the commanded, repeating commands. They call it policy. Ali was never in command. She's just made up of the hungry. She's just made up of plans.

In his desire to make capital claim its materiality Marx took Ali's. Tried to make her a leader. But Ali's prophesy was too crowded, too black, too late, too loud. Submerged in capital, the earthen buried strategy and detonated it. The first respondents told us we need to learn to be more strategic. We will learn to need strategy, they say. But we know strategy is the delivery system for a concept, collateral and deployed. Indeed, strategy is itself just a concept in the world, the universal approach. But not even capital cares. Capital only wants things to run smoothly, which is to say universally. This is what disruption is for, and leadership, and open innovation. Capital does not fear strategy. It can barely remember it from the days of worldly concepts. Marx made capital a concept. Lenin saw his chance. So capital learned to be material again. No, Capital doesn't fear strategy. Capital fears the earth's procession. Ali's blues black saint eyes.

God has everything but faith; this is why He so brutally requires ours. He looked around and was so lonely He made Him a world. Rightly, He didn't believe in Himself and, wrongly, He didn't believe in us. We were neither sempiternal nor parental, just generative and present, like a wave. In His case, (over)seeing was not believing. Faithlessness such as His demands a certain strategic initiative. Ever get the feeling we're being watched? Well, that's just God's property, the police, the ones who proclaim and carry out His strategic essentialism. They have some guns that look just like microphones. Sometimes they write books. They tell us what we need. Often, they are us. We're all but them right now but we're gonna try to fade back in and out as quickly as possible. Mattafack, let's sound it out, let's talk it over. If you could start talking over us right now, we'd appreciate it.

Nathaniel Mackey speaks of unremitting predication – what if this is our existence, given in and as a practice of chant, a ceaseless and ceaselessly inventive liturgy? You could call it the historicization of a veridical protocol in which the distinction between falsity and transformation, untruth and unchecked differentiation, is kept sacred. And it's not even vulgarly temporal in the way that seeing aspects, as Ludwig Wittgenstein describes it, implies a timeline – first it was a duck and then it was a rabbit. There is, in the simultaneity of "it is a duck" and "it is a rabbit," a kind of music. Ornette Coleman calls it "harmonic unison" and we might follow him while also deviating from him but in and through him by calling it anharmonic unison, a differential inseparability. When essence leaves existence by the wayside, what ensues, for essence, is existential loneliness. What if the problem of the concept is the problem of separation? And what is the relationship between conceptual separation and individuation? What's at stake is the convergence of the body and the concept that is given in the transcendental aesthetic. Individuation and completeness follow. On the other hand, (en)chanted, (en)chanting matter, canted blackness, (where flesh and earth converge beyond the planetary, in and as non-particulate differentiation). It's not about a return to some preconceptual authenticity so much as matter's constant aeration, its constant turning over, its exhaustion and exhaustive sounding, its ascentual and essentially and existentially sensual descent. The problem is the separation of the concept and our subsequent envelopment within it – this horrific sovereignty of the concept and its variously hegemonic representations. Did the invention of sovereignty require the concept or did the concept already bear the danger of sovereignty's brutal representation(s)?

Maybe the problem is the separability, the self-imposed loneliness-in-sovereignty, of the concept and its representations (as embodiment or individuation or subject or self or nation or state). How do we make sure that the concept still matters? How do we refuse its dematerialization, even if/when that dematerialization seems to have allowed the production of new knowledge, of new critical resources? This is a question that is explicitly for Marx. When the senses become theoreticians in their practice, in communism, which is here, buried alive, they ask questions of the one who brilliantly, and for us, both charts and re-instantiates the dematerialization that capital pursues in the separation of labor power from the flesh of the worker or of profit from that flesh in its irreducible entanglement with (the matter of) earth. Was that an instance of 'strategic thinking'? If so, it demands that we rethink strategy. Is there a way to think the relation between strategy and improvisation that alloys the maintenance of a difference between immediacy and spontaneity? There is a deliberate speed of improvisation that is not simply recourse to the preconceptual. Maybe what's at stake is the difference between movement and *a* movement or *the* movement.

Or, maybe what's at stake is the trace of perfume that has been released. It is changed in being-sensual, depurified in being breathed. There is a socialization of essence that is given in and as sociality itself and maybe this is what Marx was talking about under the rubric of sensuous activity, but against the grain of his adherence to a logic and metaphysics of (individuation in) relation. All this makes you wonder what the difference is between strategy and faith. When we say difference, here, what we really mean is caress – how strategy and faith rub up against one another in a kind of haptic eclipse, or auditory submergence, or olfactory disruption, or gustatory swooning of the overview. In this regard, strategic essentialism is something like the soul feast's homiletic share or, more precisely, the ana- and ani-charismatic sharing of the homiletic function in and by the congregation. When we say preach when we hear preaching we be preaching. It's like a conference of the birds – a constant re-materialization and proliferation of the concept; a constant socialization of the concept rather than some kind of expedient decree by some kind of self-appointed consultant who finds himself to have been gifted with the overlooking and overseeing power of the overview. The consultant's capture and redeployment of strategic essentialism is faithless and lonely. It exudes the sovereign religiosity of the non-believer. Let me tell you what we need or don't need, it says, always doubling down on you whenever it says we with a heavy, I/thou imposition, a charismatic boom that somehow both belies and confirms its sadness in the serial deanimation of its personal relationships, which is felt by us as the toxic solace of being spoken to and of by the one who is supposed to know. So maybe it's just a matter of where strategic essentialism, strategic universalism, or the concept, in general, are coming from. Unremitting predication bears a boogie-woogie rumble, where deferred dream turns to victorious rendezvous. Down here underground, where the kingdom of God is overthrown and out of hand and hand to hand, there's a general griot going on. His (and that of any of his representatives', the ones who must be representing us but can't) strategy is exhausted and surrounded by our plans.

There's a movement of the earth against the world. It's not the movement. It's not even a movement. It's more like what Tonika calls a procession, a holy river come down procession, a procession in black, draped in white. The earth's procession sways with us. It moves by way of a chant. It steps in the way of the

base, in the way of the dancing Tao. It bows to the sisters of the good foot, carrying flowers from Caliban's tenderless gardens. The earth is on the move. You can't join from the outside. You come up from under, and you fall back into its surf. This is the base without foundation, its dusty, watery disorchestration on the march, bent, on the run. Down where it's greeny, where it's salty, the earth moves against the world under the undercover of blackness, its postcognitive, incognitive worker's inquest and last played radio.

The earth is local movement in the desegregation of the universal. Here's the door to the earth with no return home and who will walk through it is already back, back of beyond, carried beyon', caribbean. Pasolini said Ali Blue Eyes will walk through the door over the sea leading the damned of the earth. Ali Blues Eyes. But we won't teach Paris to love. We can't show brotherhood to London. Ali took Trotsky's red banners and made something for us – a handkerchief, a bandage, a kiss.

PLANTOCRACY AND COMMUNISM

1.
FOUCAULT PRESENTS HIS 'TIPS' ON NON-FASCIST LIVING IN ANTICIPATION OF A cultivation of the self he may well have seen as a counter-strategy to the production of the individual.[69] But he sends his self-help text into a world of interpersonal relations, one he also documents in his account of the intimate rise of neoliberalism. Another way to say this is that he sends his text into the mouth of democratic despotism. Neoliberalism was nothing other than the completion of the Southern strategy, as Nixon and his aides refined it. The Southern strategy was of course never simply about the Southern United States. It was about the global hegemony of the planters. A global plantocracy made possible by democratic despotism. In this regard, Nixon's United States political strategy is an extension of the Dulles brothers' foreign policy, which was in turn a transnational echo of the repression of "Black reconstruction in America."

Neoliberalism sealed the global deal on democratic despotism. As Du Bois explains, democratic despotism was an innovative form of the global color line. Workers would be designated as white and offered deputy positions in the rule of each country, in exchange for aligning with the ruling classes against people of color inside and outside the borders of that nation. But in reading Du Bois we see a second dimension to this deputization, securing the deal through a promised, though always thwarted, individuation for these workers.

Or, today, for these homeowners. That is, democratic despotism was also about the democratization of despotism. We have referred to this democratization as policy. But such a hacked word should not hide the brutality of the agreement. Each of these persons was offered the opportunity to individuate through despotic violence against blackness (best understood, here, as the refusal of refused access to the unity of whiteness and personhood). Indeed, this despotic violence was the core manufacturing process of the thwarted individual. The production of white people on an industrial scale required this democratization of despotism. Of course, signing up to a world of despotism, proving one's 'self' through ongoing predatory violence against those who claim the differences they enact, required accepting the democratization of despotism as a general principle, and that meant accepting it in the military, in the state, and especially at work – as, in other words, Fordism, and later, logistical capitalism, each of which, in their own way, necessitate and manufacture a brutal little dictator in every workplace. And once despotism is accepted by white people, in and as every little ritual of their own self-acceptance, all of which amount to an endless lag, an eternal deferral, the interpersonal becomes the only way to mollify it. If interpersonal relations form the reservoir of whiteness into which the people tap for dead energy and unsustainable sustenance, then the intersectional becomes the only way for the ones who wait on waiting, whose

doubly interminable wait takes the form of critique, to mollify the constantly redoubled despotism they face. Either way, every body waits in vain.

But the interpersonal is not only not up to the task of mollification, it actually reproduces and refines thwarted individuation and democratic despotism. These are the conditions under which the Southern strategy flourished; this is the spread soil of the plantocracy. And now, the pulling down of the Confederate statue proves the strategy has triumphed. The global plantocracy reigns when the monuments walk, and rampage, like pattyrollers in the form of men. But how can we call Foxconn or Goldman Sachs planters? Because they work to fulfill the condition of any and all plantocracies. Planters try to control and concentrate all the land, all the water, all the air, all the food, animals, and plants. Pushing people into factories was just a temporary tactic in this control and concentration, not the endgame. Marxism misunderstands this. The endgame is that no one can survive outside their rule, that everyone and everything must walk into the jaws of the planter or, in other words, that the earth itself is what must be consumed. Finance is completely explicit about using its menacing means to do this. So is logistics. They are sciences of the planter. But understanding this regime as a plantocracy thriving in the individuating violence of democratic despotism does not lead to the thought that there is no outside to the world.

It leads to finding some land to share and with which to share. Because in the face of this despotism we need somewhere to really care, which is the collective destruction of the interpersonal, and with and through it the delusion of the individual, in open practices of welcome and visitation. That cannot be done in conflict with the plantocracy, where the interpersonal, or freedom, or non-fascist living, becomes our faulty weapon. It is a battle that can only be won in the militant, self-defensive, self-annihilative retreat of the new attackers. And given the nature of the rule under plantocracy, retreat means finding land that is fugitive from the rule over land, water, air, etcetera, and then setting that land up anautonomously enough to start the treatment. That land may be a squatted garage in the city or an abandoned mill in the countryside. That treatment may entail forming a band, hosting a barbeque, a dance and a drink. It may be a farm and a daycare, an experimental writing collective, or a mechanics shop. Any form of detoxification from the interpersonal. There will be no allies, no citations, no counter-portraiture. Every aggression will be massive. And when we win, blackness will rain in sun showers while the time disappears.

2.

It is difficult for those of us coming out of the black radical tradition to embrace the currently popular timeline on fascism. If fascism is back, as the common sense in Europe and the United States seems to insist, when did it go away? In the 50s with Apartheid and Jim Crow? In the 60s and 70s? – not for Latin Americans. In the 80s? – not for Indonesians or the Congolese. In the 90s? – the decade of intensified carceral state violence against black people in the United States? We don't mean to deny fascism's particular mix of lingering and resurgence in Europe, which became the supposed anti-fascist's attitude as soon the immigrant began the task of rebuilding Europe in the wake of the last of its racial capitalist self-destructions; but we do want to say something about the fundamental difference between a common life and undercommon living because we adhere to the black radical tradition's expanded sense of fascism's historical trajectory and geographical reach.

The idea of the commons as a set of resources and relations that we, as otherwise exploited and expropriated people, build or protect, manage or exploit, creates and follows on from several assumptions. First and foremost is the assumption that we could ever be anything but already shared and already sharing. Indeed, the condition of our ability to share is that we are shared. In other words, we are not individuals who decided to enter into relations with or through the commons. The commons cannot gather us. We are already gathered, as we are already dispersed and interspersed. The idea of the commons leads to the presumption of interpersonal relations, and therefore of the person as an independent, strategic agent. Such persons make not just commons, but states and nations, in this worldview.

The undercommons is the refusal of the interpersonal, and by extension the international, upon which politics is built. To be undercommon is to live incomplete in the service of a shared incompletion, which acknowledges and insists upon the inoperative condition of the individual and the nation as these brutal and unsustainable fantasies and all of the material effects they generate oscillate in the ever-foreshortening interval between liberalism and fascism. These inoperative forms still try to operate through us.

If the undercommons is not the commons, if the new word implies something inadequate about the old word, then it would be in this: that the undercommons is not a collection of individuals-in-relation, which is precisely how the commons has traditionally been theorized. We were trying to see something underneath the individuation that the commons bears, and hides, and tries to regulate. It is what is given in the impossibility of the one *and* the exhaustion of the very idea of the one. What if the practice of common life isn't about new definitions of power and new relations across difference? What if the very idea of new definitions of power/new relations across difference is nothing other than an alienation machine?

3.

What would happen if every time people used the word 'university' it came out sounding like 'factory'? Why do people think working in the university is special? The university is a gathering of chances and resources; a cache of weapons and supplies; a concentration of dangers and pitfalls. It's not a place to occupy or to inhabit; it's a place to work, to get in and out of with such rapidity and rapacious purpose that it disappears in that its boundaries disappear. All of that work ought to be securing the capacity to use those resources and to take those chances and to pass them around to the extent that they are useful. It's not a point on a line. It's not an aspirational beginning or end; it's a respirational organ that is all but certainly laced with malignancy. It requires us to consider, as if it actually had something to do with us, what farmworkers think of working on a farm, before that activity is congealed into the achievement of the identity 'farmer.' In this regard, the undercommons *is not*, except incidentally, about the university; and the undercommons *is* crucially about a sociality not based on the individual. Nor, again, would we describe it as derivative of the individual – the undercommons is not about the dividual, or the pre-individual, or the supra-individual. The undercommons is an attachment, a sharedness, a diffunity, a partedness. If we mentioned the university at all it was because it was the factory we were working in when we made our analysis.

This is all to say that the undercommons has no particular relation to, or relative antagonism with, a sector created by the capitalist division of labor called higher education. As Marx said, the criminal creates the criminal justice system. We find "informal and situated knowledge" amongst prisoners, prisoner's families, courtroom clerks and reporters, etcetera. This undercommon work is what the legal sector exploits. Lawyers and judges are primarily supervisory. And so it is with the healing work of patients and families that makes the health sector. Doctors and nurses are primarily supervisory. Beyond all the ideology of the special mission of the university sector it is worth remembering two things. First, students make the higher education system. Professors are primarily supervisory. Second, students working to become teachers, in any area, are – all of them – being groomed for management. Graduate students feel this contradiction and it hurts because they are moving from the shop floor to management. But the fact is that if you want to teach for money in our system, you're supposed to supervise. None of this would need saying if we were talking about the automobile sector. Those who work in an auto plant know their roles. If they solder they are workers. If they evaluate the quality and speed of soldering, they are management. Of course, managers get evaluated, too, and sometimes something like an appetite for being (de)graded, which accompanies the appetite for (de)grading, appears to appear. But that's small scale compared to the mechanics of "teacher-student relations," which study refuses.

Realizing that you have to supervise to teach for money, even lousy money, in our system can then lead to two forms of collective organization. We can take from the job our money and do something else together, or we can work to overturn a system that chains study to supervision because only this overturning is going to break that line. And at a certain point since any exodus both goes nowhere and undermines what it leaves, these two forms of organizing come together. Any other approach is just waiting around to be offered "supervisor of the month" or a "Distinguished Teaching Award."

Of course, part of the ideology of the university's exceptionalism is that under this capitalist division of labor the university is permitted to gather knowledge, that is, supervise not just its own sector and its students but also to supervise other sectors. It creates agronomy departments to share in the supervision of the agricultural sector, or an art department to share in the supervision of the art market, through research. But this should not fool us. It is the same for the banking sector, whose oversight and supervision of other sectors produces papers and reports.

4.

As we often suggest in conversations around the practice of study, once we try to study, the system will come for us, no matter how minor our study appears to us. And so, there is really no possibility of disengaging given the constant potential we carry to provoke engagement. Life demands we bring forth this potential again and again despite the consequences.

But engagement itself also posits and re-posits us in a way that risks trapping us in an idea of ourselves as strategic agents who have antagonistic relations with systems of power. The general antagonism admit neither strategy nor strategic relations nor strategic agents. In fact, it points to the fundamental antagonism of all *as* difference: clashing, contrasting, emerging, and fading without agents or strategies. Agents with strategies, that is, individuals, mistake all this difference for something out of which they can fashion choices, or decisions, or relations, which is also to say out of which they could fashion themselves. But the general antagonism won't let you go, no matter how hard it propels you, 'cause it's us. Your efforts at recognizing yourself and being recognized will riot on you.

This is why we find *complicity* useful. When you think about how people worry about complicity it is precisely a fear of the general antagonism. If someone is worried, as is typical, of how his art practice or curatorial practice will be compromised by complicity with the museum, or worried about how her research and teaching will be compromised by complicity with the university, at the base of that worry is the fear that they cannot sort themself out in the midst of this complicity. The person cannot say this is 'me,' my strategy, and my relation to the institution. Complicity indicates a kind of falling into something and not being able to disentangle what you see as yourself from the institution and its (anti-)sociality. The person fears not being able to say this is the boundary, fears that the border is crossing them. But no amount of strategy, decisions, or relations can disentangle us. The institution seems so much more successful than us at turning the general antagonism into the ground for individuation. But why do we feel this way when the real feeling we get from the institution is precisely the opposite, entanglement?

Now, maybe the way to deal with that resistance to the general antagonism provoked by the fear of complicity with an institution is to invoke the other use of complicity. To be complicit with others, to be an accomplice, to live in ways that always provoke conspiracy, a conspiracy without a plot where the conspiracy *is* the plot – this use of complicity can help us. This second use of complicity emphasizes our incompleteness – when you see us you see something missing, our accomplices, or something more, our conspiracy. It's all good, it's just not all there. We don't make sense on our own. There must be more of us, more to us. On our own we don't add up. And that is what we are, and that is what we are in the institution, and how we are in the institution, complicit with others who are not there in the institution, conspiring with them while inside, tangled up in the institution with the thought or the sound or the feel of the outside, which is in us, which we share in this sharing with, this ongoing folding with, this unaccomplishable *com + pli*. That kind of complicity can be deepened even as we deepen our place in, as we dig down through, the institution. We can provoke here not a strategy of within and against, but a way of living that is within and against strategy, not as a position, relation, or politics, but as a contradiction, an embrace of the general antagonism that institutions feed off but deny in the name of strategy, vision, and purpose. Our complicity refuses the purposive as its own reward and the more it grows the more the underlying entanglement of the institution overwhelms its strategy. We will have been violent to, or malignant in, the institution, cutting it together apart into nothingness, as Karen Barad might say.

Another word for this is communism. We can't be spoken of in the same breath as the League of Revolutionary Black Workers, but we can try to follow their example insofar as it doesn't seem to be the case that they indulged in a lot of hand-wringing and navel-gazing regarding their complicity with the auto industry. They didn't feel guilty or conflicted about working for General Motors. They didn't identify with GM or derive their identity from their relative antagonism with GM. Sometimes we are asked by graduate students if we feel hypocritical about being "career academics." Did General Baker – after whom, we might say, and we'd only be half-joking, the general antagonism is named – feel hypocritical about being a career autoworker? We'd rather answer such questions by saying why we can't answer them. We study with Baker and Robinson, even now, and they share how they refuse the metaphysical foundations of politics and political theory. We study with Audre Lorde and Foucault, too, but centering her pre-emption of his recognition of "the fascism in us all" doesn't rid us of the task of reading – by way of them, in their wake, under their influence and protection – against the grain of their metaphysico-political commitments to individuation, which each of them articulate by way of a certain "care of the self." What if what's always being taken care of is not this or that self but the very idea of the self that lies at the core of anti-socially reproductive carelessness? We said non-fascist living is a refusal of communism. It is. It is a refusal of complicity. It is an impossible ethics of individuation-in-relation. Individuals must, but at the same time cannot, be in relation. Increasingly, we live and suffer contradiction as the genocide, and geocide, we study to survive. *Nella complicità!*

5.

Let's imagine that Foucault shared a problem with us, and that problem was the metaphysical foundations of politics. That metaphysics says that there are individuals who bear rights and morals that must be protected by the state. Politics is the way those individuals then relate to each other, to their own selves, and to the government that emerges either from within this politics but also, as it were, outside of this politics by way of and also expressive of an authority whose foundations are not only, as Derrida says, mystical but also in and of a hard, brutal, real(ist) presence. Foucault, of course, did not believe in this metaphysics. He thought the individual, who will have been protected by the state but was in fact created by the state, was a prison house – but one created so subtly and seductively that we would open the door to it ourselves and close the door to it on ourselves. His tactic was to refuse this individual in favor of a self who would be tended to, directly, by the animate body concerned. Now, we want to share Foucault's refusal of the metaphysical foundations of politics we find ourselves trapped within. We share that refusal, in fact, whether we want to or not. That is the first sense of our complicity, that sharing, which is a sharing of and in desire. It's just that it is a sharing that is not, either in the first instance or the last, because there is neither a first instance nor a last, embodied. Sharing is, as Spillers teaches us, from within the field of black feminist theory and practice that Lorde also cultivates, a fleshly animation that moves disruptively in, while also surrounding, metaphysico-political individuation or, if you will, the body politic. We share, in complicity, that movement within that also surrounds. It is not that what we want is bound up with politics. It is that we find ourselves reduced or stayed by politics having to fight our way "back" to what is uncontained by politics. That elsewhere, where map and territory or blurred, where return fades beyond belonging, so that back becomes before, in terror and beauty, as Dionne Brand in submerged, cartographic walking, can't be found by taking the path Foucault cuts, because that path, which is the animate body's path, has always been denied to the flesh, and therefore most especially to black people who are for historical reasons violently entrusted with the keeping, in sharing, of what becomes what it always was, blackness, that anoriginal communism, which Morrison speaks of as the love of the flesh before she speaks of the care of the sources of the self and its regard.[70] Refusing the 'selves' and 'bodies' refused to them, black people live in the duress of (the state's, or racial capital's political body's) total access to – Spillers calls it a terrible availability of – what they protect but do not have, which is and must remain as the absolute vulnerability to valuation, grasp and possession of the absolutely invaluable, ungraspable, and dispossessively dispossessed. Therefore, if you follow in the swerving path of this access which must be kept open at the price of being left open, you have to, and you do, find another way.

The refusal of metaphysics we share with Foucault, that Foucault's brilliance lights in us, must nonetheless depart from his path, as it continually departs from its own in fugitive flight from freedom, slavery's preparer, accompanist, and haunted survivor. Therefore, we have to question both the metaphysics of the individual, and of relations, and, indeed, of the (inter)personal. Marx wants us to organize our powers as social powers, and he warns us that so long as we divided our social powers from ourselves in the form of political powers, we would not emancipate ourselves. But the problem extends further when we come to understand that the only conception of emancipation we can have is a political one. And so, we have to work on and for a communism that does not resolve itself into freedom or emancipation after having done all that work against the political. And the way to do that is to shift Marx's formulation under the guidance of those whose emancipation is behind them, and in hot pursuit, as Hartman shows and proves. Otherwise we would be subjugating ourselves to each other through individuals-in-relations of emancipation, the very free subjects who can do nothing but privatize, externalize, and brutalize as, indeed, free subjects always have. Instead, we can imagine an entanglement of life, and constant bloom, amid an earthy decay at which advanced, eurocriticality can only sneer in sterile and abstract disgust. We can imagine it because it happens everywhere social life surrounds the political life that seeks to separate us from our powers by offering us power, or worse, the right to demand a share of what we are forced to make and cut to meet the conditions of the demand. We can imagine it, the anoriginal communism, because it is lived wherever blackness militates against itself – wherever, as Sly Stone says, there's a riot going on. And, unfortunately, we can imagine it because the regulatory force of politics, individuals, and relations between supposedly discrete and sovereign humans, is, as Robert Johnson says, a hellhound on our trail.

6.

The act of emplotting yourself in time and space is – perhaps paradoxically at first – also the act of being all but nowhere. That spot you mapped is dimensionless. It cannot be found precisely because your act claims that the point you will have occupied is universal, the abstract point every individual can and must make and from which humanity becomes possible, with and through and in which the human finds himself. And because it is nowhere, its relationship to place is, in fact, one of impunity. It is this impunity that founds modern morality and the idea of responsibility or sustainability which this act of impunity then hires as its security detail. Can there be a better description of the human: the being who lives with impunity on the earth and is sorry about it? So, the question of what has happened can be taken with the question of what will happen in a way for which normative ethical questioning makes room. Against this abstract preparation for the victory of reason over its rivals, this tilting of the board toward one point, there is a way to live history and place that is not part of the humanization, that is to say racialization, of our earth and its reduction to world, its degradation of its means to mere logistical ends and its forfeit of sharing to mere ownership, all of which require and are instantiated by emplotment and its rule(r). Amiri Baraka calls this entanglement of history and place "place/meant" and we hear him, now, through M. NourbeSe Philip's amplification of "dis place," as if he meant for that errant and supplemental "a" to signify a movement of and in place, a radical and irreducible movement that constitutes our undercommon indigeneity, our shared, native, ante-natal turning out of (re)turn.[71] If emplotment is how we give up the undercommons for a common grave, then dis place/meant is how we find and mark the surrealistic spot.

Black imagination in the face of fascism is certainly an example of this, living history and place without succumbing fully to this emplotment; but this is not to say living in some form of life that's more 'real.' That's not the point. It's not even about the point and it's not about pointing. Some of the earliest speculative fiction we have is black speculative fiction written in response to American fascism and it's part of what is now the longest running and perhaps most successful, which is to say unsuccumbed to "success," of the earth's anti-colonial movements – the struggle by black people *all over the world* against the fascist colonial order called the United States of America. From Martin Delany to Octavia Butler, from Mary Prince to Frankétienne, emplotment is continuously disrupted in movement's names. And we could also point to the continuous non-coercive rearrangements of desire, to take a turn again with Spivak, that constitute black music, which is neither metaphor nor allegory, which is nothing but generally ante-generic black social life as it brings around its history and mashes up its place again and again.

This is what tells us that the answer to how to act is how we act. It's C. L. R.'s and Etta's future in the present, which is this train Sister Rosetta Tharpe is always talking about, that clean one Woody Guthrie sleeps on, as a pillow, with all the unscheduled calypsonians in shared logisticality; it's Gladys Knight's midnight train, the O'Jay's friendship train, Bob Marley and the Wailer's Zion train, Trane's sun ship, Sun Ra's funkadelic spaceship, the general blinds we ride. Time and space emplotment is fundamental to every capitalist production process, to all the circuits and metrics of production, beginning with the production of the human worker. Bending time and space to our offbeat beat and displaced place is bound to fuck that up, 'cause it already will. Now, if you need some, come on, get some, before it's too late. As long as you don't steal, we share.

WHO DETERMINES IF SOMETHING IS HABITABLE?

1.
Complicity is implicit in certain funky practices of the one as the common and painfully, erotically precise refusal of the political geometry of the dimensionless point. If there's a lesson to be learned, if funk turns out to teach as well as preach, it's that the proper is what gets done to the prior impropriety we share. Complicity is the already given give-and-take of incompleteness; black speech and black song are constantly trying to show you that they can't quite tell you this, a condition that is infinitely bad but just a little bit better.[72] Hip-hop is subsistence music, which spoken word insists, as radically sentimental education. It was always supposed to sound like kids playing, with kids playing, moving in and with their fleet, self-fashionably self-destructive murmuration. People trying to figure out how to make a living. People seeing if they can live somewhere.

2.
The pathway to the lived experience of impossible individuation goes through rigid conformity, whose severed, separate performances are strictly accounted for. School is where the social contract is taken out on kids. In good schools, network's eclipse of contact is enacted with great efficiency; in bad schools, an

experiment might happen, either accidentally, where networks and the networked don't apply, or under the protection of an idea of the alternative. The loss of empathy in the submission of the social to the contractual ought only ever make us want to ask, can there be cybernetic bruise? Cybernetic caress? Cybernetic sensation? This we do in remembrance of the general antagonism and the general strike we keep all but enacting, recognizing that these questions arise not from the fact of new computational hardware but rather from the values that animate old computational software – a spiritless theory of mind/hand coordination manifest most clearly in the reduction of reverent touch to instrumental grasp. It's not that touch is nonviolent. It's that we need lovingly to return such violence from resource improvement back to its multiple sources. We want to intensify our thoughtful feel of bad complicity in the interest of its brush against the good so that no one can ever say, 'Watch me make my own way through this bullshit.' The record shows, no one can take the blows and remain intact in the effort to remain intact, which is only given in the taking of the blows. If we want to fight for the good, we have to overturn the bad rather than navigate it by ourselves in crowded loneliness. It's all nappy and out of all compass – dread, naught, knotty, naughty, dred as worn cover and rent vessel. The oldness, the oldheadedness of the people, is given in their recognition and refusal of this turbulence we go through. There, they study what also can't be there. It's like a band straining against development, trying to make a music that studies it while avoiding it. Is there a point where you can't go on indefinitely? Is that space limited or unlimited? The broken document of a workshop that breaks out into poetry by breaking from the crafting of poems is a concert film. The record of thoughtful play becomes a play.

3.

"There must be the understanding that there is nothing, nothing, nothing, absolutely nothing that you can do to improve, transform, or better yourself," said Krishnamurti.[73] There is in fact nothing you can do by the false and bloody instrument of yourself. You can't hack something by yourself. You can't squat something by yourself. You can't steal something by yourself. You can't steal away by yourself. You can't steal yourself. You can't feel yourself. You can't feel bad all by yourself. And yet we feel complicit in and as 'my' individuation! We feel the need for strategy! The artist, the academic, the curator, the creative. The sanitation worker, the nurse, the teacher, the farmer. Where we work, every inch of our institutional lives is scoured and scavenged for productivity, efficiency, improvement, and profit. So, too, is our every word and act, our every thought and feeling. This navigated place without waves, without salt, is "eager to assist, organize, and structure our lifestream logistics."[74] We feel it straightening us out, uncurling us, those fingers on our scalp. And we say:

But this is not *my* improvement, *my* transformation, *my* practice. So, we try to outsmart work, outmaneuver the organization, swim against the tide. In so doing, we fall directly into the jaws of the productivity tool. Because outsmarting work, strategizing ways to be in the institution while trying not to compromise, while trying not to *feel* complicit, *is* the productivity tool. We have only to remember what we never chose to forget. The worker first produces herself, but in so doing produces not just herself but the very relations of capital. Whether informal or formal work, all work today is the work of outsmarting. That's the job. All work today aims at the creation of the individual who games, who leverages, who arbitrages, working in their crowded, solitary way. Show us someone with an abashed career strategy and we will show you a cog with feelings.

4.

But feel, which is the embrace of incompleteness undetermined by the economy of in/voluntarity, can't be subdivided into a whole bunch of anesthetized feeling some kinda way about our incompleteness. To say we feel complicit in and as our individuation is to say we feel complicit *through* our individuation. To feel complicit in the work of an organization, a profession, a corporation, is not a form of consciousness (of which the unconscious is not just one among many). It can't distinguish mental from manual labor or good jobs from bad jobs. To feel complicit all by yourself is to be a good employee. It is also to be a good citizen, to vote strategically, to make policy, to feel bad about loving your city. But to feel complicit in all our incompleteness is to be revolutionary – so much so you might even call it otherwise than being. To enter with accomplices, to work with unseen friends, to plan everyday with someone, to be with someone, is so much more than being someone in being less than someone. An individual's felt complicity with an organization is (un)matched by real complicity in feel, which is unalone. To want to be with past the point of mere being, to feel the refuge of all the rest out of sight, to have accomplices in all you do – this is real complicity, still folded, still nautical, all naught.

5.

Feeling complicit and complicit nonbeing in the feel – the two cannot live together even as they live together in our complicity. Accomplices disrupt the individuation of the complicity we feel in the organization. But the organization, too – the museum, the hospital, the school – constantly interrupts and violates the complicity we build. And yet, the more we deepen our complicit, collective, uncorrected friendships, the more the individuation machine and its "strategic career in and out of the institution" malfunction. As Robinson was fond of saying, we "deepen the contradiction." Mahalia Jackson pre-amplifies that formulation, singing about helping somebody along the way to the abolition of the efficient institution of somebody; Silva dubs it, talking about no-bodies helping no-bodies to dissolve the equations of value. As we hold on tighter to our complicities, the two can't hold. Neither can you. Neither can I. Something's gotta give and what gives is what gives. You and I are not complicit. We feel – we share – complicity.

6.

Then what's the relation between absolution and insolvency? Between insovereignty and the refusal of the absolute? Some loosening. Embrace's turning loose. It's like salvation is that present and absolute tactility of field, which is unified only insofar as it is unreachable and ungraspable. Do leaders solve or dissolve or both? Are they dissolved? Are they dissolute? Is solving to reduce? Is lysis on the way to incompleteness? Could the tragedy have been avoided if early on he'd said, "Hey fragment, don't go home"? Then it's not that we forgive, it's that we owe, which is foregiven in displacement. Every solution the kids come to dissolves – both is dissolved and dissolves the previous condition. If we were a bell, we'd say the gravity of play's inseparable from its anarchy. As a matter of fact, we go from principles to anarchy, like Martin Heidegger's better angel, Reiner Schürmann.[75] Merely to speak is to enact decomposition. When we say, "At first it was a desert, then we built a city," we slur. The half-spoken word that spoken word asks after is all about unsettling. And, interestingly, *roi* sounds just like *loi* when shouted by the abolitionist kids of Paris, our resolutely dissolute ante-republicans, who play the thread and fray and stops and frets of an idea of society. In the workshop and the playgroup there's a curriculum, a project that eventually gets let go. What the finished product will have achieved, if it is ever achieved, if it ever achieves anything, are the conditions of its destruction and rebuilding, which is the law LeRoi Jones laid gently down to William Carlos Williams in Paterson, on *Paterson*, reopening the open work to call for the end of the workshop all but before it had begun, because we play way past the point of playing and our practice is the game.[76]

7.

Adelita Husni-Bey makes films about school, art about people trying to make worlds where you can see how worlds are made. Her genre is the metatragedy (of the upgrade) of the commons. She shows people showing how the fantasy of the desert island and the fantasy of Vitruvian Man might just go together, each to usher in the other's withering. 'At what cost?' she asks them, as they ask after the cost. Vitruvian Man is *The Martian* who, in being martial, all but immediately raises, in his practical and sensuous activity, the problematic of cost and its distribution.[77] Enamored of the fertility of his own shit, he uncritically enacts the dialectic of growth and waste, saying, 'Look how I made the desert bloom.' Meanwhile, upon what is the cost imposed? We say 'what,' but not 'whom,' because the inhumanity implied in 'what' underwrites the degradation imposed upon 'whom,' who fades to thingliness or, more merely, falls to earth in the explorer's intrepid self-regard. 'Let's talk about imperialism and development,' or manifest destiny – she who was the improvement of everything – while we workshop what we workshop till it's gone. We need techniques of welcome and exclusion, sustenance and destruction, division of labor and distribution of resources, intimacy and publicness. The fantasy of the desert island kicks off a three-week developmental arc. In rapid succession we go from 'Friendship. Friendship is essential' to 'It is but not for making a tepee. Look. We need ropes, rods, and a sheet' to 'Someone must distribute the food' to 'Who votes for money?' to 'It's not a nice thing but we must punish people' to 'No king, no law.' It's as if anarchy is our end, at least in the École Vitruve, the school of microcosmography, where man is the measure of all things. There, we learn that symmetry breaks down in play and everyone is out of all compass. Perhaps the production of the Renaissance man, which is the object of a certain anarchist schooling, has as its aim the refutation of the Renaissance idea of man, who fits in a circle and a square, a globe and a map, a world and a cell, as the (empty) center of (unsustainable) gravity, a singularity grasping at the shards of its impossibility, which is what this motherfucker calls information, which this motherfucker claims as representation, which is what this crazy motherfucker thinks we are. The rigorous and critical union of art and (freshly dropped) science is messy on other planets and desert islands. It requires the anarchitectural abolition of the town hall and the deposition of performance, so we can learn that 'we gotta learn our lesson here,' since ain't 'nobody looking for us.' So, we look for us with Husni-Bey, and wonder how we turned from, and will turn back to, the infinite rehearsal that turns study mad, or black, in standing with those who have no standing until we've fallen in with them. With us. The complicit. The damned. Then, who determines?[78]

BLACK (ANTE)HEROISM

Respect

AGAINST THE BACKDROP, AND UNDER THE CONTINUED PROTECTION (EVEN IN its disappearance) of its *Wall of Respect*, conceived, painted, and dedicated in 1967, the Organization of Black American Culture allows and requires us to think about heroism. It lets us do so with a gentle, militant demand given in the way they worked, through the conditions under which they worked. And so we are compelled to say that they produced a wall of heroes and did so heroically, in the endless climate change of racial capitalism, that make our heroes as ubiquitous as they are impossible. They pass their passion on to us, they never passed us by, and we can't let that pass without remembrance. But at the risk of being misunderstood, especially misunderstood in our profound respect for OBA-C, and in our own "black hero" worship of its members, OBA-C whisper a question in our eyes: is the black hero an oxymoron? Unless we are to understand the black hero as a version of a white hero – that is, as a monument to a people that it instantiates and exemplifies – then we must suggest that the black hero somehow and against our own hearts, must be understood as unheroic, or more accurately, anti-heroic, or even (ante)heroic. Indeed, insofar as the black heroic stands in relation to the heroic it must be anti-heroic, and insofar as its formation is outside the heroic, it must be (ante) heroic. Its failure to form the relationship of hero and people makes it anti-heroic but its preservation in and of the deformation of anything as regulatory as the standing for/th of a people by its individuated and monumentalized hero marks it as (ante)heroic.

It seems clear that understanding the black hero as a derivation of the white hero satisfies only the most derivative class, the most regulative and self-regulated class. In fact, the white hero is himself derivative of a derivative, derived of a people who are themselves derived of the human, which is the category that regulates a range of differences with a mechanics of racialization which the very idea of species-being always already bears. This is the phenomenon of which *a* people are a (di)version. The white hero is erected to monumentalize a people, and to fix a part of so-called humanity in conflictual, regulatory relation with other peoples, who have their own heroes and monuments. If the hero is the individuated monument to a protocol of conflict that cannot be contained as conflict, then racialization might be held – when theories of Afropessimism rightly claim the violence of their general application – as the relay between antagonism and conflict. That relay maps onto the distinction between the enemy who, by way of conflict within an assumed equality, can become a friend, and the racialized antagonist who is given as the enemy (and, therefore, the condition of possibility) of all mankind. In the political battlefield that is so charted, the monument is necessarily a racial artifact, a regulatory fetish of a people in the figure of the individual, one and many given now in fallacious relation. Given in this way, in this derivative chain of illegitimate givens, in malls and avenues and gardens of cold, white stone, the state formation of a people riddles itself with monuments. If all the *Wall of Respect* ever did or was meant to do was reflexively and reflectively stand against that, who could object to such righteous objection? Happily, the *Wall of Respect* cuts (the metaphysical and political, racial and psychic, foundations of) respectability to the bone.

There's a telling moment in Heidegger's infamous "Rectorate Address" that is brilliantly noticed in Noam Chomsky's famous essay, also from 1967, called "The Responsibility of Intellectuals." Heidegger speaks of, and Chomsky derisively and rightly criticizes, "truth [a]s the revelation of that which makes a people certain, clear, and strong in its action and knowledge." The hero might be said to embody that truth and it is in this regard that the hero is a monument to a people. *But such monumentality cannot be ours*, a condition that requires us to consider what it is to be a people. Are black people "a people"? What do we call the everyday relinquishing of the fantasy of being a people in which black peoples have been engaged? What do we call that intense entanglement of solidarity and differentiation, which constantly and radically disrupts certainty, clarity, and whatever modality of strength that accompanies them? We want to say that the beauty of black people is in their consistent refusal to constitute a people. We move against heroism and monumentality and we need a word, or something, to correspond to the beauty and intensity of that movement. At the same time, when we have appealed to any such word, or any such something, none has ever really fit, none has ever really persisted or remained, as any successful monument should. And so we also want to say, abjuring any gesture of absolution that might be extended to the forces that erode our monuments, that the *Wall of Respect* beautifully exceeds, even in its disappearance, any appeal to monumentality.

Surely this has to do with a hemispheric tradition of muralism that links OBA-C (and their colleagues from AfriCOBRA – the African Commune of Bad Relevant Artists) to the Syndicate of Technical Workers, Painters and Sculptors in Mexico; and just as surely it has to do with the general field of relation between whiteness, subjectivity, and heroism, a fantasmatic convergence that models subjectivity in specific ways in the United States. Where common folkways erupt, under constant pressure, in the common production and reception of unregulatably differential style, the black anti-hero, or the black (ante)heroic, is given not so much in a figure as in the cutting of a figure, to use and also slightly to abuse Richard Powell's illuminative phrasing. The soloist is bas antechamber to a social practice; a continuous preface, a swinging door, a blood stain'd gatelessness, a vestibule as Spillers says, that leads to the rupture, the preservation in deformation, of black social life, by no invitation only. The individual is neither one nor everyone in this regard and portraiture, when given in such constellation, divides or shares or reconfigures the figure. Is there a prefiguration of and through the individual on the *Wall of Respect* that corresponds to the force of the pre-Hispanic in Diego Rivera's *Flower Festival*? Then this is the black (ante)heroic, whose bracketed prefix indicates that heroism isn't the right word until you put some black in front of it that can't wear off.

Dis-honor

Could it be that the white hero must fall, while the black hero must fail? This is the first sense in which those whom we love who are on the *Wall of Respect* might be honored with something more and less than heroism. They might be honored instead with a redacted heroism, an honor born not of the history of dishonor but the history of disowning honor, which is not honor's collectivization but the socialized refusal of its individuating game. That refusal of that which, according to Patterson and his forebears, constitutes (properly political) subjectivity as an effect of power and as the degradation of sociality, takes place before it is offered. Here we might index this failure to honor honor with Huey P. Newton. H. Rap Brown and Stokely Carmichael were on it, but Newton was to rise as the *Wall* fell. He was to struggle, in a double sense, through heroism. Honored as a black hero, he was an advocate of revolutionary suicide. Was this something more than dying for the people? Could it be that in the idea of revolutionary suicide, where death is part of life in common, and not its singular monumentalization, Newton suggests that the black hero does not sacrifice for the people, but *is* sacrificed for the people? Such black heroic passion bears an irreducible sociality. Moreover, what if what must die for *the* people is not only the hero but also the very idea of *a* people? The black (ante)hero is sacrificed to preserve the anticipatory and anti-regulatory deformation of the people against the grain of monumentalization and the formation of a people.

Let's approach this again by way of Afropessimism's special stringency. No slave, no world, as Frank Wilderson says; and given that this wall is erected and comes down, like its black heroes, in the world, those heroes have failed (at abolition); and so the world remains, in all its geocidally, genocidally extractive relation to earth and the differences earth bears. Such analysis zeroes in on the undeniably anheroic, the hero who fails, who fails to cohere into the monumental, who fails to instantiate any coherence of a people, as statue, statute, status, or state. She would appear, most devastatingly, as never to have been erected, never to have been torn down, as unable to fall in having always already fallen into abandon and dispossession.

This analysis washes the wall for further revision of the black (ante)heroic, for preservation and priority of this washing away, this washing over and under. Robinson writes about the preservation of the ontological totality. It is his answer to how something that should have been impossible, given the laws of the hero and his people, nonetheless exists. The ontological totality is a conjuring of collective African being at the moment of struggle, at the height of insurrection, and even at the point of death in battle. But crucially and excruciatingly it is impossibility that forms its condition as unconditional deformation. The Africanness of the ontological totality is therefore more and less than African and otherwise than being. Its preservation requires its opening, its incoherence, its refusal to coalesce into anything like a people. It is, in other words, not African but Pan-African. Terribly, beautifully, terribly, beautifully, it is foregiven to us and in us to be given away, such dispersion itself being the opposite of the heroic and more in the direction of the profanely, pandemoniously sacrificial. What's continually sacrificed is the soloist in the soloist's continual appearing, his constant showing up to be sacrificed and dispersed, preserving the experiment by failing its monumentalization. This is black art's unbearable brutality. Albert Murray can't quite get to how fucked up it is in *The Hero and the Blues*. No blackened existentialism, no shaded tragic consciousness will do. Nevertheless, Nanny Grigg or Nat Turner, Robinson teaches us, keep something going through their certain deaths, keep something going that cannot win under the rule(s) of the hero and his people, but survives in something more exhaustive. There is something unheroic about this, the failure to win, and something other than heroic about it, too. Under the law of the hero, even tragic heroes are remembered despite their own fall or death through the victory of *a* people. They are monumentalized for having fallen on the road to success. Or, at least, this is the way a white hero is conceived. But the black anti- and (ante)heroic is condensed and dispersed in sacrifice for the victory of *the* people by the ontological totality in its antagonistic relation to *a* people. With the help of OBA-C, AfriCOBRA, and AACM (Association for the Advancement of Creative Musicians) – can we imagine another way to think about the soloists, about the women and men we call black heroes, about certain blacks who groove on love. What did they do, what did they render, beyond the heroic and unheroic as it comes to us in this world? Asking these questions, which loop back to the question they ask us, means looking close enough to hear more in their work, and their way of working (through the work), and the place where their work went on.

Everyday

We notice again, when we keep trying to pay attention, that OBA-C, the street gangs, the tavern operator, the neighbors, survived under daily conditions that we might otherwise say, but should not say too easily, gave rise to the heroic. The place where the work went on and the people who did that work emerged from black social life, from the impossible everyday, conducted daily. Everyday people live (ante)heroically in the world of denied and refused peoplehood. In the space around the *Wall*, the strained superlative, the broken perfect, the impossible under generalized conditions of impossibility, are on from can't see to can't see. In heroism's burdened, burlesque corrosion, we see the quality of the quotidian deed, its constant revision, its common condition, its disruption, its unmonumental apposition. But we have to resist taking away from this unmonumental apposition the idea that everyday black people are heroic, and instead, without denying that idea, focus on its surround: that the black (ante) heroic is (a constant variation on the) routine. It's not so much that daily life is infused with heroic deeds, but rather that heroism is reworked, or unworked, as daily collective social life; that is, as prosaic, repeated, revised, varied, experimental, discontinuously restarted. All that crowdedness and rub that happens on the Wall is given again and again in all that happened to the Wall. There was first and foremost what Romi Crawford calls "a being present and around the Wall." There were plays put on and music played in front of it. Parts of it got painted over, it all got rained on, it supported incalculable drama; a dead body was left propped against it, the FBI took pictures of it, it got burnt. The Wall's eventfulness is sometimes portrayed as what it went through – a sign of the times and symbol of the place. But, really, that *was* the Wall, not what it went through; that's what OBA-C was, and their anti-heroism existed in service to the black (ante)heroic, as everyday commitment to the annihilative provisionality of being that was, at the same time, total. If we look at photos we have of the painting, and hear the poetry around the wall, and the music, we encounter again and again antagonism, painting over, house paint and white wash, cardboard and string, as well as a total commitment to the impermanence of form because form is to be used, like an everyday thing. You use it, that is to say deform it; you use it without owning it, without permission to use it; you don't keep it for a monumental occasion but preserve it, in letting it go, in acceding to and enacting its transformation, in and for the everyday.

It was never about this or that person being seen; it was always about this or that person being seen through. Nor was it ever about seeing through the special hero to his or her variant from around the way. That's not seeing through opacity, that's mirroring given in transparency. But the Wall's transbluesency, the amplified delta haze it still gives off, let's us misrecognize, pulls our coat to how recognition of the everyday hero threatens the preservation of this ontological totality. It parries and deflects that being-subject to reaction precisely because the bestowal of heroism in the interest of telling the truth of *a* people rings false in the impossibility of its relation to the people's black and open generality.

In other words, the aim of the wall was not *its* preservation, which will have never forestalled what we might call its disappearance, but, rather, its transformation precisely in the interest of the preservation of the ontological totality. In this it differs from the monumental. Nor was the aim, strictly speaking, the preservation of the heroes against the general anti- and (ante)heroism that sent them. Nor, and finally most importantly, was the purpose the preservation of a people, their monumentalization. What OBA-C gives us is the deformation of a people in the name of something else, something stranger and more beautiful – a general antagonism with species-being.

The Wall and its histories help us see that a people is just a regulatory reduction of *the* people; and a person is simply the sign of a people or, better yet, a people's unit of value, pegged to the hero in mutual impossibility. This reductive formula bears the national(ist) subjection of the people's weirdness, the constant differentiation of which – in and as undercommon practice, in and as irreducibly haptical and topographical social poiesis, in and as study – will have been rendered coherent by means of arithmetical separation. This is how nationalism and individuation go together, how there can be this seemingly paradoxical combination of national character and the absolute singularity of persons, since weirdness has to be individuated, and then collected, in order to be calmed. The monument, which is an extension and intensification of the logic of the portrait, is the crystallization, resolution, and/or embodiment of this paradox: the national individual in the glory of a general equivalence he stands for, simultaneously abstract and unique – the representative man as a kind of currency, the coin of the realm. But differentiation is neither individuation nor pluralization. It refuses the law of the integer. Go to any bar to see this weirdness under duress, on display, as it tries to defend itselflessness. Go to a black club, or church, to see how this is done with the greatest and most delicately violent technique, preservation given in an immeasurable range of dispersion and disbursal, as our romantic disposition, our mantic deposition, our antic apposition. We so crazy we tore up our own monument – kept rubbing it with the furious questions it taught us to ask, kept submitting it to the terrible enjoyment of our condition, until it disappeared. Mackey might say that the *Wall of Respect* is another instantiation of our "eroding witness." In this regard, black nationalism is anti- and (ante)nationalism, just as black heroism is anti- and (ante)heroism. That's the African pan.

Washing our work

Now, what might this mean for those of us who want to walk in the footsteps of OBA-C today, which is to say in the footsteps of the black radical tradition, and in the footsteps of everyday black social life as the collective honor to refuse honor, the black (ante)heroic? Well, we've always had black heroes. So, what does it mean to render them in our work, in our writing, with this understanding of the (ante)heroic? How do we do that? Does it mean, with OBA-C, we have to find ways to demonumentalize our work and the work we write or paint or sing about? Is it unfair to say that current cultural form, insofar as it has been adapted in black artistic and intellectual life, places black study at risk to monumentalization, seeks the heroic, pulls away from the black (ante)heroic?

One version of this monumentalization is the amount of honor bestowed on individualized position. Spillers speaks of it as the ruse, or the lure, of personality. The mere presence of the black scholar, the black artist, the figure who would cut the figure, is taken as a victory to be preserved, rather than as an effect of a compromise forced on cultural institutions by the movement of black people and forced on the movement of black people by the powers that operationalize cultural institutions. When we allow this to happen it is not just that this mere presence in the institution assumes a model of heroic representation of a people, but also that this attitude seeks to regulate what that movement might really wish to make disappear or wash over amidst these derivations of appointment and position. There is no culmination, in individuated units, of the people.

On the other hand, taking OBA-C, AfriCOBRA, AACM, and others not only for how they inspire us but for how they undo us, how their (ante)heroics preserve the chance to undermine the temptations of the monumental and the lies of the hero and his people, we can perhaps start to help each other disappear, paint over one another, play over ourselves, let our solos fade into our noise. The *Wall of Respect* was at the service of an undercommon flight from being, and fight through being. It was not the object. It did not merely stand against. Its objection flourished under and around its objecthood. And so long as jobs and shows and books are the object (seen as necessity rather than their necessity being seen and lived through), we will be heroic. We have to find new ways of working that insist on the impermanence of the monuments in exhausted, inconsistent totality. How can we make a living that way? How can that way be our living? It will have been more than a reversal of all we do, though it is that; it is a sacrifice which no one of us can even volunteer. Sacrifice – to share in offering, in pleasure, in mourning, in remembering – is often, now, regarded as obscene, while the single claim upon station is lauded as a virtue. Black virtuosity, black heroism, had better be something bad!

SUICIDE AS A CLASS

In "The Weapon of Theory," Amilcar Cabral says that the petty bourgeoisie are best placed to take over after colonialism in part because this class does, indeed, have an understanding of imperialism. After all, who would feel more keenly the denial of personhood, which imperialism administers as politico-economic instrument and effect, than those who feel they are most proximate to it? Who is more aware of the unbridgeable distance between themselves and personhood than those who suffer the constant and brutally apparent nearness of this impossible subject and object of desire, which imperialism imposes with such diabolical rigor? In a complicated way, both in and against the grain of Cabral (and Septima Clark and Frantz Fanon and Elma Francois and Fred Hampton and Claudia Jones and Paule Marshall and George Padmore and Funmilayo Ransome-Kuti and Walter Rodney and Barbara Smith), we have grown accustomed to the unspoken notion that those who are so poised speak most naturally and effectively of and for the anti-colonial impulse and aspiration. But when Cabral says so clearly that there is no contradiction between having an analysis of imperialism and being part of the petty bourgeoisie, and when he suggests so emphatically that such an analysis is an essential feature of the petty bourgeoisie in and after colonialism, and when we remain aware of the labor the petty bourgeoisie does in the construction and maintenance of colonialism and imperialism in and after colonialism and imperialism, in the countries and peoples who continue to be subjected to them, where aftermath and immersion are consubstantial, we might be able to accept the chance – which Cabral offers us – to reconsider our habits. This is a chance for black study to deal with a problem fundamental to black study, which appears at the advent and in the ongoing evolution of black studies, where revolution and devolution are way too close, in comfort.

If we speak now, hopefully under Cabral's protection, of the neo-colonization of black study by the academic-artistic complex, it wouldn't be to point fingers, either at others or ourselves, but to try to think, in our tradition, anindexically, in loving discomfort, in the common rub. Consider, then, in the interest of a sometimes necessary timeliness, the current flare-up of the ongoing battle between native and immigrant in the Afrodiasporic quarter of the United States academy, which is less like *Game of Thrones* and more like *Gangs of New York* insofar as at the end of every day we're left with the sad phenomenon of a petty bourgeois elite play-fighting amongst themselves while black workers try to make some air to breathe. That air is, and has always been, enjoyed more by their petty bourgeois counterparts than by black workers in the oppressive, genocidal atmosphere of the ongoing and ever intensifying fascist counterinsurgency of whiteness.

Consider, too, that there are no more time-honored and useful categories for the production, reproduction and protection of imperial power and its operations – and for the suppression of peoples' and the people's capacity to move, and to rest, both in refusal of home, all irrespective of national borders or identities – than native and immigrant. This is especially true in the United States, whose variant of North American whiteness has always been a noxious mix of these false alternatives. The scraps from this bloody manufacture that are left to non-white petty bourgeois subject citizens, whether they want to claim or disavow becoming-American, consists of fragments of one or the other but never the fullness of both, that wound resolving into a black scar on a white mask, liquidating undercommon differences in the name of cold imperial separation of and within black social life, both in the United States and all over the world that the United States dominates with ever more murderously slapstick venality. Meanwhile, the petty bourgeoisie works hard, if often unintentionally, to protect the metaphysical foundations of the very imperialism it critically understands. Its performative intellectual reflexes pass for a fantasy of subjectivity that is predicated on their inability to have it. The petty bourgeoisie claims to speak – from a position it assumes but cannot avow – for those who discover the oxygen it can barely produce; it claims to breathe for those who can no longer breathe; it claims to be here, now, for those whose presence was never so easily plotted. It does this unintended, immaterial labor with the best of intentions while postcolonial malaise is visited not upon actual imperial power but upon the petty bourgeois intellectuals themselves – unwitting, and even unwilling, compradors who 'choose' the moralistic (out)rage for rhetorical purity that 'decolonization' has become over the endless, fugitive, anti-colonial struggle for the survival of ante-colonial life, which is running out of time, as it always has.

The intensity of the trouble lies in that shit like this happens amongst *us*, the good people of every rotten, brutal, delusional nation-state. Every single person who isn't really one, and knows why they aren't and can't really be one, means well when they speak for those for whom such personhood was less an object of desire and more a ghostly matter to beware and avoid and destroy. Hell, we mean well right now, hoping there's something in what we say that pierces what we assume in saying it. It's just that such hope is nothing without practice, such faith is nothing without work, without toil, without that constant, active, undergrounding labor whose by-product will have been our disappearance. This is the content of Cabral's prophetic description. He sharpens the weapon of theory for us so that we can cut through theory and ourselves. He gives us a chance to see more clearly that the competing chauvinisms of native and immigrant, when the color line constitutes the interdiction of their convergence, obscures intra-diasporic, intra- and international class warfare in every outpost and refuge of Afrodiasporic life. The lives and struggles of Negro toilers remain to be thought, and inhabited, as the unswerving apposition of the unthought, the unhabitants' fugitive deconstruction of world and reconstruction of earth. The weapon of theory lets us see through to the social lens we want to see through when we are Negro toilers, too.[79]

In this light, we might begin to understand the decolonial petty bourgeoisie's strange incapacity to self-nominate either as a class or as revolutionary while proffering an all but constant critique of imperialism. It turns out not to be such a mystery if we move in the way of analytic description, refusing the opposition of description and analysis while working way off to the side of self-description and self-analysis, as well. Maybe analytic description begins with the awareness that there has to be more to it than analytic description, which is not in and of itself para-ceremonial practice. Black critical reflexivity can't simply declare itself to have escaped the hall of mirrors that constitutes (self-)representational mind and its political arts. What it will have been to publish has to open onto a kind of devotional incompleteness rather than incompleteness's disavowal. What sisters will Cabral have been grounding with, sharpening the weapon of theory 'round a kitchen table in the absence of a kitchen?

What if the absence of the kitchen is a function of something that will have been there? Note the title of Cabral's famous speech. He uses the phrase "weapon of theory" because he is making an argument for theory. He is coming so far from the other side that he feels he has to make this point. He is coming so far from practice, or more properly, from praxis, from so far outside the house, where the absence of the kitchen makes the kitchen table possible, that he feels like he has to remind his audience that theory is a weapon and that it is *our* weapon. He's coming from the farm where he's done soil analysis, and the tent where he is planning an attack in common defense, in and also out of and also off of these groundings, and saying theory is not just theory but also a weapon. Now, consider how utterly superfluous that phrase sounds today in/to the academic-artistic complex. Of course, theory is a weapon, we often hear. It's our weapon of choice (but also of deferred necessity, of necessary deferral). But this rallying cry of theory as a weapon, heard all but everywhere on the biennial and triennial byways and at every gathering of the institutionalized faithful, has lost the content of the words Cabral uttered at the first Tricontinental Conference of the Peoples of Asia, Africa and Latin America in Havana in January, 1966. He told us theory is part of the arsenal of revolution; he didn't say that it was the representation of revolution or a possession of the ones who represent.

But today, what is this rallying cry, "theory is my weapon"? And from what practice does theory emerge within the academic-artistic complex? It emerges from a practice in which theory is reduced from a realistic spot of common seeing to an abstract, unoccupiable point of individual expression. It is no wonder that this complex is as tautological as the military-industrial one, which ensures our safety by making the world more dangerous, enforcing precarity in the name of security. Cabral says we are not gathered here to shout at imperialism. That is not how this weapon works. And the main reason it does not work like that is functional, not theoretical. Theory cannot be wielded by a theorist. It cannot be lifted or aimed alone, by a single voice, or even by a chorus of single voices shouting at the enemy. That's how our weapon gets pried from our own dead, individuated hands and is deployed against us – on the bodily remains we call our own and act like we walk around in – as an instrument of torture and shame. That's not a revolutionary weapon. Now, when we think about what such a weapon would be, the practice of revolution having come more fully into relief in the obliteration of whatever delusions of repair we had (which will have always been directed, finally, at the system that breaks rather than those who have been broken), we have the proper reason and the proper tools to get a sense of the importance of what the petty bourgeoisie, which today can be said to include the branch managers, shop owners, independent contractors of the academic-artistic complex, can and cannot, must and must not, do.

Famously, Cabral says that once it has taken power, "the *revolutionary* petty bourgeoisie must be capable of committing suicide as a class in order to be reborn as revolutionary workers, completely identified with the aspirations of the people to which they belong." Moreover, he says, "national liberation is essentially a political problem, but conditions for its development give it certain characteristics which belong to the sphere of morals." Cabral doesn't here say commit class suicide. He says commit suicide as a class. For what if the very idea of class suicide is the deferral of suicide as a class? What if that final act of class will, undertaken by another subject of history substituting for the one – the proletariat – that just won't ever act right through all its unconcealable lumps or residual lumpenness, is nothing but a final, endlessly recrudescent act of politics, in and on its terms of order and metaphysical completion, where state and subject, in the deadening and anti-differential merger of the individual and the collective, dance their decaying mutual orbit? No, Cabral says commit suicide as a class, which he says will have emerged as a moral problem when we analytically describe the political scene correctly. What if the correct analytical description is one in which class recognition, given in the denial of a constantly enacted class status, is displaced by a constant, experimental exercise of antagonism wherein the economy of mis/recognition is abandoned? At stake, here, is less the commission of a collection of individualized acts and more the omission of the metaphysics that reduces undercommon practice to politics, which is nothing but the act of the individual. What if the moral problem emerges from its subsumption in the political problem when power is neither taken nor democratized but is, rather, refused? Class suicide is a (set of) political act(s); suicide as a class is anti- and ante-political practice. So that the realm of morals, contrary to popular and scientific belief since the West started trying to give birth to itself, and then started trying to secure itself by enclosing all that it determined – in various processes of hyperrational delusion – was not itself, is not the space/work between subjects in relation. Note that this (dis)solves the old problem concerning the very idea, let alone (im)possibility, of political morality or moral politics. Morality and/or ethics and/or aesthetics doesn't operate in the imaginary space between subjects (and objects). Practical, antipolitical refusal of the metaphysics of class 'morals' are a matter of murmuring. To feel fully the aspirations of the people to which you belong would bring about a terrible and beautiful differentiation in murmuring, an harmonic irresolution of and with and in the choir, in anticipation of a shift in flock, where belonging is in flight from belonging in sharing, at rest in an unrest of constant topographical motion. The weapon of theory is a conference of the birds. The kitchen table is its public and its publisher.

Let us try to expand, with greater precision, on how suicide as a class – the refusal of class and its structures and rituals of membership, which include the simultaneous enactment and denial of class identity – operates outside the distinction between (acts of) commission and omission. Remember William Munny in *Unforgiven*? He says, "It's a helluva thing killin' a man – you take away all he's got and all he's ever gonna have." Well, what kind of thing is suicide? What is suicide's relation to consent's non-single non-being? The massive work of autodivestiture implies an even more massive practice of mutual aid, where analytic description folds over into or rubs up against communal practice. Perhaps one must go through the hell of having become justified in murder as a response to the brutal disruption of xenogenerosity, a dispossessive availability, in which case murder, or self-murder, is the subject reaction, which is part of the self-indulgent, self-determinative, self-deceptive, nationalist, statist, neo-colonially decolonial program of the petty bourgeoisie, which can always be asserted either from the self-styled immigrant's or the self-styled native's position. If national liberation – as it moves through the discourse of self-determination – is a political problem then that is also the extent to which it ought not be our problem, however much it gives us problems, we who live and/or want to live the life and struggles of Negro toilers who, in their contour, in their voluptuousness, in their uneven grounding, in their note-bending, shout-twisting lumpenness, have no class (as Marx will have affirmed with unerring but unhearing insight, as the Panthers knew). Their nonmembership is a practice of nonbelonging.

Now, we can consider (the political problems of) the people who consider themselves the 'revolutionary petty bourgeoisie.' Of course, the first problem is that no one so considers themselves. This Marxian class category is now used primarily in the service of a weird anti-communism while old bourgeois categories like 'middle class' or 'professional', or new ones like the 'precariat' or the 'creatives' are casually deployed, functioning – in the name of 'analysis' – as non-analytic descriptors of components in a static system. It is equally unclear that this "class that will not call itself a class" considers itself revolutionary, or at least that members of this self-denying class would use this word in public to describe their outlook, much less their daily activities, with a few exiled exceptions. Nonetheless, there exists a class that does not call itself a class, and will not publicly describe itself as revolutionary, which does indeed have an 'understanding' of imperialism that could be called revolutionary and which, moreover, recognizes itself in that understanding, as the bearers of that understanding and, more importantly and more deludedly, as the continually renewable end of that revolution. What are we to make of this telic dehiscence? First, perhaps deferral is a better word. The deferrals of not "being as a class," and of not declaring "for or of the revolution," prevent what would be analyses or descriptions of imperialism from having one fundamental consequence, in particular: suicide. On the other hand, they also raise a deeper question: why would we even want this petty bourgeoisie to commit suicide? Or, more pointedly, why would we even want them? Do we require what we desire, which is not from but rather for the petty bourgeoisie, who at least appear to be accomplices in anti-imperialism/colonialism if not in revolution, a contradiction in which they (with)hold themselves? Finally, the question is, what do we want from and for ourselves? Do we suffer a failure or a surfeit of self-consciousness as a class? How do we refuse this strange self-conscious acting out of the class unconscious of the revolutionary petty bourgeoisie?

The point here is a nagging one. Maybe it was wrong to propose that the petty bourgeoisie might make the choice to commit suicide as a class. Newton is working on this problem with his idea of revolutionary suicide. He seems not to require the entirety of the class but at the same time to seek some way for that partiality not to fall into individualism. His is not simply a vanguardist asceticism – that the leadership must 'die for the people' – but rather an understanding of the way the petty bourgeoisie could have it both ways, or in other words, how the petty bourgeoisie were/are a true class, operating between the bourgeoisie and the workers. This was the class Newton met in Oakland as his father took him around when it was time for people to pay the monthly bill for the household furnishings they'd bought on time. He saw the durability of a class of local collectors, gathering the evilly distilled wealth of the neighborhood and thereby playing the indispensable role of distinguishing the workers and the lumpen through the function of management and finance; he also saw through mere analysis, which is, in itself, held as comfortably in the hand of policy as a mace or a pike; he saw through what Cabral called the structure of "ownership in society," which never overlaps directly with the ownership *of* society, to which the furniture dealer, the furniture manufacturer, and the professor lay claim.

Of course, Cabral constantly puts this to the petty bourgeoisie in no uncertain terms – you better make your choice. But Newton saw that this deferral of revolution – given also and with the softest but most certain devastation in the being of a revolutionary class for itself and for others, whose ethics are constantly rehearsed in anti-imperial or anti-racist or anti-trans/homophobic acts or stances or sentiments or intentions – *was* the fundamental material condition of the revolutionary petty bourgeoisie. When a member of this class says something like after I get tenure, or after I publish my book, or when I get promoted, or once the kids have graduated, or in my second term, or when I start my news blog, this doesn't indicate strategic miscalculation or a personal flaw, or cowardice, or immorality, no matter who says such thought crimes should be punishable by cancellation, a sentence often uttered and carried out by the etymologically challenged ones who claim to be against incarceration. However, saying such things, and cancelling the ones who say such things, comprise the fundamental condition of being in that class, even when those who defer fool themselves into thinking they have arrived and even when those who defer have an analysis of their constant non-arrival, having arrived at never having arrived being the ultimate deferral of suicide as a class.

Thankfully, Cabral reminds us that the anti-imperial petty bourgeoisie is a real, though not eternal, class. It is real because it is produced in the evolving mode of production. Logistical production distributes management. It does not reduce or dissolve it. It is now all up and down the art market, for instance. Self-management or authorship is the misapprehension through which petty bourgeois class power operates. In any case, a part of this petty bourgeoisie now lives in a suspended condition of deferral and separation fifty years after Cabral while making its analysis every day. But maybe this was always its real condition, which was always also its false condition. Because if they did somehow commit suicide as a class, if that were ever their shared practice, they wouldn't just realize that revolution is already here, they would 'exist' as nothing other than the revolution, as and in its militant preservation, like Negro toilers.

Meanwhile, how does analysis, like policy, as policy, sort the revolutionary petty bourgeoisie, the workers, and the lumpen and how, and why, is this left in bourgeois hands, not as a function but as a prerogative? How does this legacy militate against what Martin Luther Kilson Jr. saw as happening in some instances and needing to happen in all – a preferential option (as opposed to the talented tenth who are supposed to bear and exercise it)?[80] How did imperialism's opposite come to be framed as anti-communist? As freedom? As the individuated thought: 'What is the point of denying to myself what they (you know, them, the white bourgeoisie, the *real* bourgeoisie) have given to each other?'

There's another speech in which Cabral addresses government employees still working under the Portuguese administration of the colony. He urges *them* to join *their* struggle, saying, "Every employment should become a combat post." If every job is a combat post, then every post becomes partisan, as it is. What if the preferential option is nothing but the common defense against the present option, against every employment deployed against us – including self-employment, including self-care's refusal of self-denial, which is the essence of just about every job, given in a vast range of mixes of self-exaltation and self-degradation, so that every fucking job is the worst fucking job you could have, a condition you can fight by yourself neither on nor off it. Sorry, Godfather, but ours is not to own the job. We have to fight the job. We have to fight the terms and conditions, the exclusions and separations, that subordinate our work to their job. Theory must be our weapon in that struggle and it must be given in our practice, in how we gather, along our way. Because it's really not about what we say if that saying doesn't emerge from and recede into the work we do. No individual act, or collection of individual acts, of expression, which is what even armed resistance is reduced to in the institutionalization of memory, can represent, let alone wield, the weapon of theory. To bear such arms will have been given in the practice that we share and defend, bearing, militantly caring for our differences in common, which is outside any structure or economy of class individuation's political morality. In the name of an ethical socioecology, in the hope of a general refusal of being petty, this is the revolutionary bourgeoisie, over and out.

THE GIFT OF CORRUPTION

This is *Natures nest of Boxes*; The Heavens containe the *Earth*, the *Earth*, *Cities*, *Cities*, *Men*. And all these are *Concentrique*; the common *center* to them all, is *decay*, *ruine*; only that is *Eccentrique*, which was never made; only that place, or garment rather, which we can *imagine*, but not *demonstrate*, That light, which is the very emanation of the light of *God*, in which the *Saints* shall dwell, with which the Saints shall be appareld, only that bends not to this *Center*, to *Ruine*; that which was not made of Nothing, is not threatened with this annhilation. All other things are; even *Angels*, even our *soules*; they move upon the same *poles*, they bend to the same *Center*; and if they were not made immortall by *preservation*, their *Nature* could not keepe them from sinking to this *center*, *Annihilation*.
– John Donne

1.

Black peoples preserve and defend the invaluable for everyone while not fully having access to it themselves. This paradox is made more severe by the fact that this non-full, non-simple access is given, and withdrawn, in black peoples' practices. Moreover, and consequently, their partial access provokes the unlimited duress and brutal resistance visited upon them from and in the world, which presumes, and seeks to enforce, total access or none at all. So that what is accessed – what is retained and guarded; what is conserved, as Humberto Maturana says – is what Chandler and Andrew Benjamin might call the anoriginal displacement of an ingrained, dispersed indigeneity, which is the only kind, in unlimited variation. It's like when the world is not looking, or perhaps we should say not seeing or hearing, which is always and all but never, black peoples pull out this invaluable little all we need and work on it, play with it, love it and hate it, hand it and never let it go. But this aesthetic sociality, as Laura Harris calls it, is curtailed, and not just by white supremacist, capitalist devils; somehow, also, black peoples can touch it though it's out of reach, listen to it though it's out of earshot and see it though it's gone. This nonsensical – Okiji has called it non-sensual – feel is the keeper's curse, the giver's chance, the fade that can't be faded.

Focus on the term or theme corruption has always been off. It's as if we were corrupted by corruption's corruption from the start. Mackey speaks of Baraka speaking of John Tchicai's playing as always "sliding away from the proposed" and this sliding, this glissando, this gliding up and down, or maybe from side to side, along the scale, this disequilibrium, this immeasure, is already there in the word corruption. It's there in the way that 'corruption' can't protect itself from what brushes up against it in a kind of semantic swarm: decay, impurity, fallenness, sin. Corruption can't protect itself from the outside that's already inside it, as its very essence, to which we have fallen victim insofar as we were already that essence's very emanation. Who are we to speak of corruption when we are its very gift? Since we have fallen, and we can't get up, all we can do is try to get down with corruption; but very soon, this seems like stealing, and not just stealing away. Corruption is, in one way, about how things fall apart within the general problematic of things never quite coming together and this thing we are doing, this event, is right in that mix, or midst, or mist, or mystery, all all or nothing up in here, all out there as a general tendency.

The gift of corruption is an afformative fantasy; an ante-static, metamorphological fade. The first way we try to come at this thing we're already in that's already all up in us as our own essence and undoing is through John Donne or, as we like to call him, in mistranslation, John Gift, or John Give. A big part of what Donne gives, of what gives in Donne, of the general donation that is given in Donne's vicinity, of what yields there, especially, in the late work of the divine known as Donne, is a massive meditation on death, that ever-emergent occasion. The problematic of death is, for Donne and in his eschatology, inseparable from that of birth and, more generally, creation. So, all we have to offer you now is leftovers. We'd abandoned something we wanted to write, for Stephen Booth, about "Meditation X" from Donne's *Devotions Upon Emergent Occasions*. From Donne, we keep learning and unlearning some things about preservation, which Booth calls conservation. The book these scraps were supposed to be in has long since come out, but we preserved them even though they had already gone bad, or off, or been partially used. We still want to offer a reading of (the) meditation's calypsonian allure, its ruminative thrall, the way not being able to get over it or leave it behind induces going against its grain. Maybe close attention to the grain *just is* against it, resisting it, or exciting its resistance. Do we want a resurrective poetics? Maybe the general practice is textual ecology, and what we're trying to see and hear is what has no value, what cannot be improved but only put to use, again and again, in a kind of decline, a kind of fall, in decayed orbit's strangely preservative spiral. Again and again, there's nothing to be gained, so you could call it preservation and uselessness, as Booth might do, but with some withering, Withersian feeling good about the expenditure.

Maybe the resurrective, when it's all tangled up in a revolution that Fanon prophesies, is just this utterly naked, consubstantial declivity. Maybe imagining so short of and beyond demonstration, will allow some investigation into the nature of personhood, its internal constituency, syntax and brutal grammar. Maybe it will be possible to get at something like the divinity – given in their uselessness, given in the refusal of being put to use and, at the same time, in the embrace of being-instrument – of manmade things or unmade man. But we should be more precise and say that we're not interested so much in offering a reading of Donne, or of considering Booth as a reader of Donne. (Does Booth even like Donne? There's a vestibular feeling that Booth values, an experience of being on the threshold of discovering what is not quite there, a potential for potentiality in "a mind just before it seizes on the witty connection of disparate things" that Donne, one suspects Booth would say, too often takes away, before its having been given, in the grandiosity of his gift.[81] Maybe there's too much flashy self-congratulation, too much heraldry, in Donne's wit. Maybe there's not enough held in reserve so that its fleet non-appearance can be discovered. Maybe Donne doesn't leave enough unmade, too boisterously and wittily calling our attention to what we should unwittingly experience; maybe he leaves nothing to preserve in the simple, incalculably complicated act of pointing to that which will have never quite happened.) But perhaps in his ostentatious generosity, Donne provides some insight into the kind of thing that Booth does in his criticism, all in the interest of amplifying announcement.

The preservation of *potenza*, of what hasn't happened yet; *the preservation of the tendency*; the conservation of subjunctivity that is given in the figure of the quark, the unit of matter/energy that stands at a distance from what Booth calls "active, substantially informative ambiguity" and which, in so doing, makes possible the specific kind of (inter)articulation that Booth says makes for poetic greatness ("the interaction of exploited and latent energies"): this serial reference to the point and moment of discovery is the way Booth's work unfolds; this is the irritating gentleness of his "close reading without readings," the insistence with which he rubs texts the wrong way, tasting their Eucharistic presence, as it were, in a certain radical misunderstanding of the host. There's an anaphenomenological refusal of the statist impulse and one is reminded that there are things, even in this world, that subjects don't make, as if worldmaking itself were predicated on the assumption that even it could be relinquished with a kind of earthy joy.

2.

What's the relation between sense and death or between sense and the state or between explication and interrogation, between these and torture? Is criticism's incessant rub what Samuel Delany would call a "game of time and pain"? Is this the flipside, the terrible aside, of suspension, of a certain textual ecology of error, of earthly life in/as world's underside and apposition? What if the purpose of criticism is suspension – literally staying in the air, keeping or holding shit up in the air, holding it up like Ali held up Floyd Patterson or Ernie Terrell – every punch, augmented by the verbal accompaniment of an endless quiz consisting of a question that could not be answered ("What's my name?"), become a structural support keeping upright what has already been felled by the serial lecture that has been read, applied to it like a strap. This would be an action akin to the experience of the lunar athlete whom Booth says we all become when we read Shakespeare's sonnets – but the difference is that it is not only the text but also ourselves that are not given to but placed in this spiraling levitation where falling always feels like flying, where reinforcement is nominative violence. This is the aggressivity of Booth's conservatism – in preservation as an act of irruptive, corruptive in(ter)vention – a torturous activity and acquisition of finding/s where magic remains magic only insofar as it is explained.

Of Ben Jonson, Booth writes:

> The couplet's inclusion of reminders of uncomfortable ways of thinking about the child's death gives a still-platitudinous and simplistic gesture the feel of a philosophy that has been tested and found sufficient.
> Let me explain.

Nonsense reinitiates a problem of philosophical translation as well as sufficiency: *Sinn*/sense/meaning is or are brought into play precisely insofar as much of what Booth does when he preserves nonsense – when he reveals it, explains it, valorizes it – is keep open or keep opening referential suspense in its endlessly eccentric fall. This is how *Sinn* and sin, sin and corruption, rub each other the right way. This is also about transubstantiation's descent into consubstantiality. What is it that a text becomes for us, through ritual, in having been announced, like the real presence of Christ in the Eucharist? It makes you want to run: from the devotions, the trinity, and ternary form to the nonsense of a broken circle. When Donne is coupled with Henry Dumas you get a kind of Trane, whose meditations, and those of Mingus, all touch on the intra-action of nonsense and spiritual sustenance. What is it to be nourished by the insubstantial? Is there a materiality of the insubstantial? Maybe that's what literature is. But if it is, if it's the doing of that work, then it is so in and as the gift of corruption. It's as if when the words, "this is my body, take it and eat it" are uttered, then what's in dangerous and overwhelming proximity to the promise of resurrection is the problem of insurrection. In Donne's meditation, this shows up as a world and body problem, a problem of corporeity and institutionality, which Jan Potoçka's *Body, Community, Language, World* helps to illuminate. There he writes:

> We arrived at the conclusion that the world in the sense of the antecedent totality which makes comprehending existents possible can be understood in two ways: (a) as that which makes truth possible for us and (b) as that which makes it possible for individual things within the universum, and the universum as a sum of things, to be. Here again the phenomenon of human corporeity might be pivotal since our elevation out of the world, our individuation within the world, is an individuation of our subjective corporeity; we are individuals in carrying out the movements of our living, our corporeal movements. Individuation – that means movements in a world which is not a mere sum of individuals, a world that has a nonindividual aspect, which is prior to the individual. As Kant glimpsed it in his conception of space and time as forms which need to be understood first if it is to become evident that there are particulars which belong to a unified reality. It is as corporeal that we are individual. In their corporeity, humans stand at the boundary between being, indifferent to itself and to all else, and existence in the sense of a pure relation to the totality of all there is. On the basis of their corporeity humans are not only the beings of distance but also the beings of proximity, rooted beings, not only innerworldly beings but also beings in the world.[82]

Now, who is this "we" Patoçka is talking about? The "we" who have arrived at this conclusion? Well, we are the world, in a sense. We are the world insofar as we can arrive at conclusions about the world – more specifically, the conclusion that world is what makes possible for us truth and individuation. The world is our common corporeity, its institution, as it were, within which our individuation is given in and as the body, that individuation rolling back into and on and as itself as the condition of possibility of knowledge of and in the world. We are the we who are the world insofar as we are and have (some) bodies. But this steady state system, in which body and world are given as one another's condition of possibility and preservative, is burdened by the anti/biotic dynamism it is meant to contain.

If the concepts of the body, and the world, are born in and as a kind of mutual embalming, wherein philosophy overlooks that upon which theology must ruminate, then Donne's rumination is given as a constant, residual freak-out over the fleshliness that neither the body nor its theft, neither the concept of the body nor its juridico-philosophical withholding, can contain. Innerworldly beings' bear but cannot bear Kafka's "inmost intensity;" underworldly nonbeings bear questions made of a disembodiment Fanon finds unbearable. If the concept of body, and of world as some kind of collective epistemic body politic, amounts to some kind of mummified institutionality, it does so within the context of a constant speaking of corruption, a constant, self-directed charge of corruption that actually constitutes a kind of embalming. In this regard, anxiety over corruption preserves the body and, the body in, the world. We speak of our corrupt institutions so they can be reformed; to speak of our corrupt institutions is, in fact, to reform them. This is how the interplay of so-called public relations and so-called investigative reporting becomes pseudo-democratic self-congratulation, wherein the institution in question refuses to decay, to disintegrate, to deform. More precisely, what's at stake is not the reform of institutions but the deformation of the institution as such. How will this have been enacted? Through something like militant preservation. But this is where it gets tricky – in the redoubling of corruption's innumerable little edges.

Corruption is the impairment of purity. Its roots are in a verb that means, to break. The routes of those roots are unmoored, mangrovic and immeasurable. One follows them to the entanglement of generativity and decay, then disappears. What if the very concepts of body and world are each the embalming of the other? What if militant preservation is inseparable from a kind of decay? Then we would have to be concerned not only with what corruption does to the institutionality that kills us, but also what it does for us in the name of preservation. *The paradox of political corruption is that it is the modality through which brutal institutionality is maintained. The paradox of biosocial corruption is that it constitutes the militant preservation of a general, generative capacity to differ and diffuse.* These paradoxes combine to gild the edge of corruption, turn it towards a gift, which was already double-edged, which we might wear, or don, as if it were the very fabric of our skin.

To don, to do on, to put on, as in, "Did she put on his knowledge with his power?" is to bring to mind one of the words Donne most loves to put on: "apparel'd." He speaks, for another instance, in "A Lent-Sermon, Preached at Whitehall, 2/20/1628," of what it means to apparel our meditations with words, of how such clothing of the thought in words, which is inseparable from that clothing of the word in flesh that is our savior, and that piercing of the flesh, that covering of the flesh in feel(ing) that is our salvation, all constitute a necessary chain of decay configured as miraculous remonstrance. To dress, to array, to make up or make over is how salvation shows itself to us, gives itself for us, and it is how and that we show ourselves to salvation in gratitude for and acknowledgment of it. But showing, this interplay of appearance and what it is to be apparel'd, is also given in and as our fallenness, our sinfulness, our unowned partiality, from the very beginning. Donne speaks of us as having been, in spite of our natal nakedness, apparel'd in sin. Sin as habit, as costume, is our very birthday suit, so that what is most authentic to us, this fallenness that is what is innermost to us, becomes our outer wear. We come into the world naked, unclothed, wearing nothing but our sin; but, as Donne says, "Sin is so far from being nothing, as there is nothing else but sin in us." That's how meaningful we are.

Meanwhile, is din, which is, as Glissant says, our discourse, the sum of sin + don? Is our damned foregiveness – this terrible practice of having been there before in being gone, in going off – the revolutionary gift that passes through us, or to which we are appended as leaves to or in a common wind, so that we are carried by what drives and pierces, so that we accompany the breath we bear in our dispersal, in how we share not being in a fade or fringe or soufflé of ash? Is fallenness - which is our fleshliness, our monstrosity, as gift - just this entanglement of entanglement and decay and survivance that attends being held and touched and handed in this tendency of pending, as if all we are is just this continual being broken by and broken off, inseparably? Is this principle of incompleteness in common, of being clothed in naked skin, of being apparel'd in sin, of having donne'd our flesh in a general, atmospheric intra-vulnerability, only to be claimed through being lost, through being stolen, in being shared in tight dis place/meant's interminable delay? We've always been attuned to the fact that we're dying here, that we're dying all the time, in this survival that we share. We've always been despised for that attunement, in survival, to survival in passing on by this (mad)Man who wants to live (apart) forever. Surveillance will have stayed us so he can stay and try to stave all off in stealing everything. But somehow being-held escapes the hold's epistemological and politico-economic grasp and works disruptive refusal of the normative politico-economic discourse on corruption. That discourse disavows corruption, projects it onto a new world, or a third world, while it is reduced to the fixed operationalization of an inveterate and brutal stability that constitutes the globalization of normative political economy. Neoliberalism's relation to corruption is, in this regard, like Pat Boone's relation to Fats Domino. What they call corruption is, really, a form of politico-economic embalming. A mummification of the dead body politic against the degenerative and regenerative force of social existence.

What we're after is the difference between submissive and militant preservation, and that between reformative and deformative corruption, when divinely violent nastiness moves in the service of itsselflessness. Is sin nothing other than this preservation's and corruption's gnostic tangle?

Sin, they say, is the act of transgression against divine law. But if, within a Christian eschatology, we are always already fallen, our orbit already given, as it were, in decay, then our illegality is a natural condition. Here is where what Robert M. Cover calls the jurisgenerative principle, in all its fecundity, comes into play as an inveterate para-legality that is not only against but also generative of sovereign legality, as something like what Derrida calls the mystical foundations of authority. Well, it's something like more or less + more + less than that; something anafoundational, something anarchic, something like nothing at all. Sin is also errancy; it is to miss, to be off track, to be off the mark, beside the point. Can it bear the sense of being unfixed, displaced; and is, therefore, fallenness given here, in this regard? Heidegger distinguishes fallenness from sinfulness but they brush up against each other, here. In the discourse of hamartiology, our errancy can either be detached from Adam's insurgency or irretrievably and irreducibly given in it; but either way there is still what remains unaccounted for and unaccountable in his tendency, which was already waiting on us, pending, appended, apparel'd, given in the folded incompleteness, the literal invagination of his body, which is not his in being that by which he's borne, that errant service that every story of origin tries to forget. It's not that Eve is Adam's corruption; she ain't his mama, or his baby mama, either. Rather, she is something like a resonance that lies before, and inside out, as the principle of an inseparable difference to which he can be said to have belonged, as belonging's dispersion. It's like a homeomorphic cup that runneth over into where hold and whole are given in their mutual exhaustion.

It's like the first moment of rap, which is music's corruption, is the first moment of music, which is the first time someone shouted "Corrupshion! Ruckshion!," so the people can dance.

3.

The state is the regulation and oligarchization of corruption, the wealth of holding what is given and letting the given go. The continual corruption of the body, of its boundaries, the continual enactment of living as this sharing matter with the environment, is what the state was b(r)ought to steal. The state regulates sharing for the purposes of privatization; it commits (to) impoverishment in the name of value. So that what is called corruption in the political world, or the development world, would be the metastasis of the state as a regulator of corruption. Then, anti-corruption drives are re-regulatory drives, designed to re-deliver the regulation of corruption, or to fail to do so; in either case, it is our corruption that suffers at the hands of the vain attempt to privatize a piece of it, or isolate a moment of it in our ongoing entanglement. The regulation of and extraction from our corruption (including through pre-emptive logistics or surveillance) has to straighten out our kinky, curved, and matty, massive, unlocked flesh. It cuts one path through our tangled rendezvous, for watching. And what if surveillance isn't a legal and extralegal category but an economic one? And what if corruption is a way not only to think the unity of political economy but its insufficiency, too? What if to strip the earth/flesh we have donned is to watch and disentangle the senses for the impoverished, non-renewable pleasures of capitalism, where enjoyment itself must be supplied through empty time? But this may simply be to say that blackness, and usually black people, deliver this kind of capitalist value whether in a recognizable economic category, including social reproduction, or not in one, through corruption. Surveillance then becomes a form of value extraction. And what is that form? The sucking of a sense, the shaving of a share, the culling of a curl, the dividing of a din, made possible by temporary, unstable isolation in the regulation of corruption. The mummification of pleasure won from the regulation of corruption, which they always lose, which always gets lost, in our eyes and arms. So, the policy question concerning the depth of your state's corruption is really the constitutional question concerning that state's capacity to regulate it.

When the state regulates corruption and tries to keep it from those who come from it, what if it's merit that it puts in our way, blocking our paths with its own single file? They tell us meritocracy and corruption are opposites, but maybe state-sanctioned, state-regulated, state-conceptualized corruption is just a tool of meritocracy. So, how can we corrupt that? Well, we have to start by saying that everyone will tell you that they know society is not a meritocracy. It's just that we can't stop acting like it is. We know this from our job (but not our work). To be a university teacher is to know your workplace is not a meritocracy. No one is there on merit. The classroom is not like a can of Narragansett. It's neither 'sold on merit' nor 'made with honor.' Nevertheless, merit is constantly invoked, if not directly then through the rules, which are designed to enforce it. Students want grades. Faculty members want tenure. They deserve them, or they want to earn them, because they need them. The language of merit is all around us, which is another way of saying the imposition of scarcity is everywhere, in part because we constantly invoke it in our defenseless defense. But merit doesn't decide which of us gets the limited resources at hand. It grounds limitation itself, creating scarcity one individual at a time. Why is there not enough to go around? Because each must have his own. But who's got his own? No one, which is to say that meritocracy is its own lie. It imposes individual evaluation for purposes of individuated distribution but it takes the form of creating bands and classes of merit. A's and B's.

At least when kids argue about who the GOAT is they know it's ridiculous, that the only way to decide would be to pound everything that is different out of each GOAT to make the ranking stick, so that the first difference to go would be the difference of every GOAT from whatever individual is called the GOAT. But that's what we do in education. So, when we say that meritocracy is the imposition of scarcity, we mean that it is the imposition of the scarcity of difference, all things being equal in this nightmare of equilibrium.

It's true, as Paolo Do notes, that the university is no longer simply a fortress. It's a consultant, too, though this doesn't mean that the university is just handing out the means of production to anyone. There's a trick to making the means of study seem scarce. All the work that goes into imposing a determination – of who gets admitted either to 'teach' or to 'learn' of who gets to sit in class, of who gets to publish, of who gets to get credit, to be qualified, to graduate, to pontificate – enacts, operationalizes, and enforces the fantasy that the means of study are not general and degenerate – corrupt, corrosive, transformative – as generativity's share. And students, faculty and deans are – as the deans would say – aligned here, all things being equal in scarcity. In this venal in/equality, everyone believes in quality, in excellence, in measuring who is good and who is better. Everyone believes in creating individual units for purposes of comparison, distribution of resources, and restriction on the means of knowledge production. Faculty perform constant surveillance and evaluation on each other under the rubric of merit, deciding how purportedly limited resources are parceled out to the purported individuals of varying merit. Everyone agrees to the rules protecting merit, and appeals to those rules, especially the ones like us, who are critically astute enough to say that, of course, there is no meritocracy. Because the rules keep things from becoming too corrupt. This is how merit is not the opposite of regulated corruption. They work together against us, especially when we try to work them on our own behalf. So that all too often, we work them together against ourselves. Any call for transparent or noble leadership in the university – or any institution, any museum, any city government – is a call to the rules of meritocracy, a call to make things scarcer, starting with the things we use to make things – the means. There's a similar trick in Singapore. Singapore's clean government is not a function of its meritocracy (rich families run the place like most places); it is instead a genuinely highly developed mechanism of imposing scarcity – highly developed because it achieves so much consent. Many Singaporeans believe hard work will be rewarded. The reward is graduated and calibrated access to Singapore's wealth on the condition of accepting and embracing, just like many faculty members and university students, severe restrictions on the means of production. Another way to put it is that strong institutions regulate and restrict corruption *as* a means of production, forcing us to develop when we really want to be sedated, or wine up on somebody nice nice nice, with a Narragansett.

So we turn, again, to Duncan and Schrödinger:

> Our consciousness, and the poem as a supreme effort of consciousness, coms in a dancing organization between personal and cosmic identity. What gnosis of the ancients transcends in mystery the notion Schrödinger brings us of an periodic structure in *What is Life?*: "...the more and more complicated organic molecule in which every atom, and every group of atoms, plays an individual role, not entirely equivalent to that of many others." "*Living matter evades the decay to equilibrium,*" Schrödinger titles a section of his essay of 1944. "When is a piece of matter said to be alive?" he asks, and answers: "When it goes on 'doing something,' moving, exchanging material with its environment."
>
> What interests me here is that this picture of an intricately articulated structure, a form that maintains a disequilibrium or lifetime – whatever it means to the biophysicist – to the poet means that life is by its nature orderly...[83]

And then to Gary Zukav and Werner Heisenberg:

> Probability waves as Bohr, Kramers and Slater thought of them, was an entirely new idea. Probability itself was not new, but this type of probability was. It referred to what somehow already was happening, but had not yet been actualized. It referred to a *tendency* to happen, a tendency that in an undefined way existed of itself, even if it never became an event...
>
> This was something quite different from classical probability. F we throw a die in a casino, we know, using lassical probability, that the chances of getting the number we want is one in six. The probability wave of Bohr, Kramers and Slater meant much more than that.

According to Heisenberg:

> It meant a tendency for something. It was a quantitative version of the old concept of *potentia* in Aristotelian philosophy. It introduced something standing in the middle between the idea of an event and the actual event, a strange kind of physical reality just in the middle between possibility and reality.[84]

We turn to them to turn through them in speculation and the play of the informal; for the enforming, subsistent existence of life; as material-environmental exchange past the point where exchange, environment and the environed maintain their separable sense at the expense of material soul; up against the partition of ideality and actuality, where and when the event is in recess; with consensuality's unravelling of the conceptual surround; toward thoughtfulness in measure, which refuses either to exclude or be grasped by measurement, which remains irreducible to itself insofar as measure is what it can neither exclude nor grasp; under song, as they say, or the poem, which fade into music and poetry fading into sound and sound, which is speech's slur and ante-origin. All that is just our run-on itinerary, out here where tendency meets touching, feeling, and terrible availability in a sense or *Sinn* or sin Eve Sedgwick + Hortense Spillers understand.

Yesterday, which now is many days and many years ago, Zo wanted to look at pictures of the old house in Los Angeles, of himself as a baby and a little boy. He smiled and said "he's so cute," and started crying, already aware of something gone or passed, feeling it more deeply, always, than the ones who want to grow up. There's no intention to rise to the form but through it, on the other hand, in an unpredictable tendency to do, whose realization is constantly refused in the neighborhood of the neighborhood. This is just the tip of an intuition, through practice, through study, which scholarship or scholasticism, in spite of its merit, holds, like a depth charge, in its heart. This is just to say again that the evasion of the decay to equilibrium of which Schrödinger

speaks is not the evasion of decay in general. It is, rather, the preservation of that decay, which bears the answer to the question 'what is life?' in natal and fatal occasions that never quite come into their own, that are themselves always evaded, where what it is to split and what it is to come just rub and rub and rub as a general, generative tendency that we can call nothing other than poetry, as long as you call it that wherever you see it, which is everywhere. What if poetry just is the corruption of language and what if that corruption corresponds to sociality's corruption of community, flesh's corruption of body, and earth's corruption of world? Then the meaning of life is its sinfulness. Their corruption is not us. Our corruption is not theirs. Blackness is the meaning of life. Partial, held secret, held out to all but not all there for those who hold, not ours and all we got and here it go, all incomplete.

HOME IS WHERE WE DISPLACE OUR SELVES

Zun Lee

We came to know each other in war, and in war we continue.
– Subcomandante Marcos

I want to make this a special tribute
To a family that contradicts the concepts
Heard the rules, but wouldn't accept
And womenfolk raised me
And I was full-grown before I knew
I came from a broken home.
– Gil Scott-Heron

I'VE HAD A COMBINATION OF NEARSIGHTEDNESS AND ASTIGMATISM FOR AS long as I can remember. No pair of eyeglasses managed to completely correct my blurred vision. Things got so bad in sixth grade I had trouble deciphering what the teacher chalked on the blackboard, and my school grades dipped. Aaron (I called him Dee), a soldier from a nearby army base, was my father figure then, one of many GIs who temporarily inhabited that kinship throughout my entire youth.

I remember spending one afternoon up in Dee's room at the barracks. We listened to vinyl records he had recently purchased and looked at photos of him when he was stationed in Okinawa. Many were out of focus, and due to my vision challenges I couldn't quite figure out what I was looking at so my frustration built quickly. I'd move the images closer to my eyes – so close they almost touched the tip of my nose – then I'd move them away from my face again. Neither made a difference.

"No, you gotta be close to the picture," Dee interjected. "Stop moving the photos back and forth. Stay close. Your eyes are off anyway, just let it all blend together." "I'm doing it but it doesn't work." "What do you see?" "Fuzzy shapes and colors." "Good. Close your eyes." Dee proceeded to narrate every detail in each photo, creating a rich, vivid world out of places, people, and things. He'd even ventriloquize dialogue if a frame depicted some kind of human interaction. "Can you see this now?" "Yeah. It's like I'm right there with you."

"Now listen to this sweet head voice," he said, as the final minute of Deniece Williams' song "Silly" played, her delicate soprano soaring to impossible heights. "In Japan, they call her kind of voice yellow. She sounds yellow to you, right?" "Not sure what you mean?" "Her voice is yellow like the sun!" "OK, I think I get it. But to me, it's more golden like a sunflower." "Good. But don't get smart with me now. And don't let nobody tell you that you can't see!"

Over time, this chromatosonic interplay of attending to color with sound and to sound with color, this rub between "not-really-seeing" and "seeing beyond," has permuted any and all ways of sensing and feeling when I create. My practice reflects a desire to get close – physically, emotionally, affectively, spiritually – and to share this experience with my collaborators. I'm less interested in "re-presenting" and more in a kind of holistic "re-presencing."

With the idea of syn(chron)esthetic blur swirling in my head for this book, I went through my entire archive to find images I hadn't gotten close with in many years. I eventually rediscovered a photo I made in March 2011 on a subway platform in New York as the 2 Express train rattled by on the opposite track. What emerged somewhat in focus were the MTA posters insisting "Improving, non-stop." Everything else dissolved into a motion blur.

Almost decade later, in the midst of our pandemic exhaustion (let me be clearer: a pandemic of continued neoliberal extraction disguised as institutional solidarity statements, token diversity initiatives and reform-as-ersatz-abolition dialectic), the image invites a deeper engagement: The subway system as a metaphor for algorithmic logistics, an infinite assembly line of essentialized workers serving continuous improvement (and being continuously improved upon), with the process itself being "improved nonstop" to move the contained, containerized, shipped ever-more efficiently. But the blurred form also suggests something in excess of that, a refusal to be straightened, a syncopation in the rhythm that kills, a collapse of our ordering in spacetime, of the linearity of space and time itself. What if we allowed this train (and ourselves in it) to derail, to deviate from its emplotted path? What is possible when we are dissolved to be able to travel through nothing into nothing, from all-access and no block toward non non block?

A dissolution, a derailment, is how I'd summarize the unsettling effect your essays had on me. Rather than using photos as mere illustration, I chose images that themselves can be read as unsettled texts, in direct conversation with the fugitive texts in this book. Many of the files hid on a hard drive covered in dust, yet they still expressed the spirit in which they were made, a personal rebellion against the constant straightening imposed on us.

My early days as an amateur street photographer (amateur in the very sense of 'someone who loves') reflected a desire to enact an energetic exchange, borrowing from the world, even if for a few seconds, and returning something back to it. Discussing these images with friends on social media was an integral part of that practice. Together, we made a photograph something more than a visual object, our virtual sociality became part of the frame. Unencumbered by institutional rules, our online photo jam sessions seldom focused on the visual. We refused the constant push towards aesthetic legibility and mastery exerted by the art-academic-industrial complex. Continually regenerating the insurgent expression of our lived experience through photography enabled us to feel our way toward otherwise narratives of survival. We understood that a photograph we cherish always moves with, in and through us; it never actually freezes time and space.

What institutions (art schools, museums, galleries, publishers, curators, artists) seek to freeze, however, is a subject reaction that separates an individuated photographic object from its equally individuated and shameful 'voyeurs,' producing a never-ending need to credentialize our legitimacy to make, show and talk about images: Since our own knowledge about us is never deemed enough to describe what a photograph means or what a good photograph is, we must subject ourselves to be straightened by institutions that proclaim to know better than us.

But what if, through our entangled, incomplete sociality, we could engender this blur of/as 'always forming but never completing' to dissolve the imposition of photographic subjectivities particularized into the distinct perspectives of the maker, sitter, viewer, seller, buyer, teacher, critic? Can we dodge and blur an algorithmic syntax that straightjackets and atomizes us into total access, so we can get back to rebuilding our atrophied habits of assembly? Can we do all of this in homeless homefulness, a perpetual displacement arising from undercommon generosity in shared spaces that belong to no one in no time, that we can only inhabit by constantly dislocating ourselves?

A daily practice to engage these questions has always been at the core of my lived experience in the general antagonism. Some may consider the idea of such insurgent hapticality too idealistic, too romantic or too insignificant. But I can point to that afternoon with Dee and countless other moments of sharing, however short-lived, moments too wild, too queer, too ungovernable to simply reinforce the structures and conditions of ontological precarity. There's always a "beyond," always a "more than" which fosters social wealth and unlikely microclimates of care. That doesn't mean the matter of how we survive and thrive isn't still the most urgent, most immediate concern – we cannot wait for a tomorrow that will never come. We have always figured out, in the here and now, ways to stir up ripples of daily care that expand into tidal waves of fugitive power. We often don't practice blurring the dots between quotidian reality and future possibility, but that shit's been real for me. I'm the product of such care in the hold. I wouldn't be here without it although I know I'll meet the same premature fate as all of my kinfolk who didn't/won't make it.

The online plenum we inhabited a decade ago disintegrated with the sale of the social media host. Our motley crew dispersed onto other platforms but a similar ensemble of the corrupt never regrouped. For many, collecting likes has replaced fostering love. Gaining followers outweighs cultivating co-conspirators. Algorithm-induced doomscrolling exhausts our capacity to care. So imagine my joy at your generous invitation to make something different and to be able to learn with and from you. Joining you felt like gathering with old friends who remind you of your 'oom boom ba boom' when you have long forgotten. We renewed our habits of assembly although (or, because) we cannot physically come together right now.

Thank you for reminding me that our real purpose of 'making' is to encourage possibilities for presencing in and through experimentation. That study is wake work toward incompletion, so we may more tightly interconnect the tender synapses of our callused souls. That abolition starts with the self, so we may lose our individuated selves in favor of a blurred, irreducible sociality of the senses.

Enough with worrying about what they say or do. May this be an open invitation for more friends to join in the incompletion of this fucked-up world. Let's keep making something different. Together. Now. We all we got. And 'all' is all we gotta be.

ENDNOTES

THE THEFT OF ASSEMBLY

1 Shoshana Zuboff, *The Age of Surveillance Capitalism: The fight for a Human Future at the New Frontier of Power* (New York: PublicAffairs, 2019).

2 We draw this short biography from a much more detailed and illuminative text. See, Michael A. Barnett, D.A. Dunkley & Jahlani A. H. Niaah, ed., *Leonard Percival Howell and the Genesis of Rastari* (Mona: The University of the West Indies Press, 2015).³ Édouard Glissant, *Poetics of Relation*, trans. Betsy Wing (Ann Arbor: University of Michigan Press, 1997) 12.

3 Édouard Glissant, *Poetics of Relation*, trans. Betsy Wing (Ann Arbor: University of Michigan Press, 1997) 12.

4 See May Joseph, *Nomadic Identities: The Performance of Citizenship* (Minneapolis: University of Minnesota Press, 1999) and Vijay Prashad, *Everybody Was Kung Fu Fighting: Afro-Asian Connections and the Myth of Cultural Purity* (New York: Beacon Press, 2002).

WE WANT A PRECEDENT

5 Cedric J. Robinson, *The Terms of Order: Political Science and the Myth of Leadership* (Chapel Hill: The University of North Carolina Press, 2016), 196-97.

USUFRUCT AND USE

6 Tsenay Serequeberhan, "The Critique of Eurocentrism and the Practice of African Philosophy" Emmanuel Chuckwudi Eze, ed., *Postcolonial African Philosophy: A Critical Reader* (Cambridge: Blackwell, 1997), 143, 142.

7 Georg W. F. Hegel, *Elements of the Philosophy of Right*, ed. Allen W. Wood, trans. H. B. Nisbet (Cambridge: Cambridge University Press, 1991), 88. Emphasis in original.

8 Ibid., 376.

9   Ibid., 90. Emphasis in original.
10 Ibid.
11 Ibid., 91.
12 Bryan Wagner, *Disturbing the Peace: Black Culture and the Police Power After Slavery* (Cambridge: Harvard University Press, 2009) 1.
13 See Cedric J. Robinson, *An Anthropology of Marxism*, 2nd Edition (Chapel Hill: The University of North Carolina Press, 2019 and *Black Marxism: The Making of the Black Radical Tradition*, 3rd Edition (Chapel Hill: The University of North Carolina Press, 2021).
14 Conversation with Jeff Mao at the Red Bull Music Academy, quoted in Matthew Trammell, "How to Stay Cool as Fuck Forever, According to George Clinton," *The Fader*, May 14, 2015, http://www.thefader.com/2015/05/14/how-to-stay-cool-as-fuck-forever-according-to-george-clinton.
15 Jacques Derrida, *The Politics of Friendship*, trans. George Collins (London and New York: Verso, 2005), 306.

LEAVE OUR MIKES ALONE

16 Anthony Wall, *Upon Westminster Bridge*, BBC Television, 1982. See https://youtu.be/NE3kVwyY2WU
17 M. Jacqui Alexander, *Pedagogies of Crossing: Meditations of Feminism, Sexual Politics, Memory, and the Sacred* (Durham: Duke University Press, 2005), 328.
18 See Denise Ferreira da Silva, "No-Bodies: Law, Raciality and Violence," *Griffith Law Review* 18(2), 2009, 214.
19 Nahum Dimitri Chandler, *Toward an African Future – Of The Limit of the World* (Living Commons Collective, 2013), 81.
20 Paolo Freire, *Pedagogy of Freedom: Ethics, Democracy, and Civic Courage*, trans. Patrick Clarke (Oxford: Rowman & Littlefield, 1998), 58.
21 Chandler *op. cit.*
22 See Barbara Smith and Beverly Smith, "Across the Kitchen Table: A Sister-to-Sister Dialogue," in Cherríe Moraga and Gloria Anzaldúa, ed., *This Bridge Called My Back: Writings by Radical Women of Color*, 2nd Edition (Kitchen Table/Women of Color Press, 1983), 123-40; Tiziana Terranova, "Free Labor: Producing Culture for the Digital Economy" in Marc Bousquet and Katherine Wills, ed., *The Politics of Information: The Electronic Mediation of Social Change* (Alt-X Press, 2003), 99-121.
23 Ah Kee also writes in *Whitefellanormal* (DVD, 30 sec, 2004): "If you wish to insert yourself into the black man's world, his history, in his colour, and at the level at which you currently perceive him, then know that you will never be anything more than mediocre." I want to thank Rachel O'Reilly for bringing Ah Kee's work to my attention. See her "Compasses, Meetings and Maps: Three Recent Media Works," *LEONARDO* 39(4), 2006, 334-39. See Essex Hemphill, "When my brother fell," in Essex Hemphill, ed., *Brother to Brother: New Writings by Black Gay Men* (Washington, D.C.: Redbone Press, 1991, 2007), 137. Hear Luther Vandross, "Power of Love/Love Power," *Power of Love*, CD, Epic EK 46789, 1991.

24 We're thinking, here, of a collaboration between Theodore Harris and Amiri Baraka, *Our Flesh of Flames* (Philadelphia: Anvil Arts Press, 2008).
25 Mary Pat Brady, *Traffic: Density's Resistance to Scale* (Durham: Duke University Press, forthcoming).
26 For more on Savoir-faire see *Klondike Kat #1*: https://youtu.be/qAXZb7qLKp4

A PARTIAL EDUCATION

27 Michel Foucault, *Discipline and Punish: The Birth of the Prison* (New York, NY: Penguin, 1991), 334-337.
28 *Ibid.*
29 See Ruth Wilson Gilmore, "Golden Gulag: Prisons, Surplus, Crisis and Opposition," *Globalizing California* (Berkeley, CA: University of California Press, 2007) and Jordan T. Camp, *Incarcerating the Crisis: Freedom Struggles and the Rise of the Neoliberal State* (Berkeley, CA: University of California Press, 2016).
30 Denise Ferreira da Silva, "1 (life) ÷ 0 (blackness) = ∞ − ∞ or ∞ / ∞: On Matter Beyond the Equation of Value," *e-Flux Journal* 79, February 2017, available online at http://www.e-flux.com/journal/79/94686/1-life-0-blackness-or-on-matter-beyond-the-equation-of-value
31 Etta James, "All I Could Do Is Cry," Chess Records, 1960, written by Billy Davis, Barry Gordy, and Gwen Gordy, https://youtu.be/3Pc9BmXN998.
32 Jack Halberstam, *The Queer Art of Failure* (Durham: Duke University Press, 2011).
33 See, for example, on the demands of instruction for employment, Franco "Bifo" Berardi, *The Soul at Work: From Alienation to Autonomy* (Cambridge: The MIT Press, 2009).
34 Luther Ingram, "If Loving You Is Wrong," Koko Records, 1972, written by Homer Banks, Carl Hampton, and Raymond Jackson for Stax Records, https://youtu.be/rmiuAUnT_tQ
35 Samuel R. Delany, *The Motion of Light in Water: Sex and Science Fiction Writing in the East Village* (Minneapolis: University of Minnesota, 2004).
36 Arthur Jafa dir., *Dreams Are Colder Than Death* (film, 52 min, 2014) http://arika.org.uk/events/episode-6-make-way-out-no-way/programme/dreams-are-colder-death
37 Foucault, *op. cit.*
38 See, for example, on endless demands of employment, Peter Fleming, *The Mythology of Work: How Capitalism Persists Despite Itself* (London: Pluto Press, 2015).
39 Maria Josefina Saldaña-Portillo, *Indian Given: Racial Geographies across Mexico and the United States* (Durham: Duke University Press, 2016).
40 For a superb examination of the couple and the heteronormative family as extensions of individuation see Melinda Cooper, *Family Values: Between Neoliberalism and the New Social Conservatism* (Cambridge: Zone Books/The MIT Press, 2017).
41 Cedric J. Robinson, *The Terms of Order: Political Science and the Myth of Leadership* (Chapel Hill, NC: University of North Carolina Press, 2016).
42 Silva, *op. cit.*

43 See Fred Moten's discussion of synesthesia in the essay "Amuse-Bouche," *Jacket 02*, February 2, 2015, available online at https://jacket2.org/article/amuse-bouche, accessed May 21, 2017.
44 Alexis Pauline Gumbs, *Spill: Scenes of Black Feminist Fugitivity* (Durham: Duke University Press, 2016).
45 Hortense Spillers, *Black and White and in Color: Essays on American Literature and Culture* (Chicago, IL: University of Chicago Press, 2003).
46 See also Fred Moten's discussion in *In the Break: Aesthetics of the Black Radical Tradition* (Minneapolis, MN: University of Minnesota Press, 2003).
47 Saidiya Hartman, *Scenes of Subjection: Terror, Slavery, and Self-Making in 19th Century America* (Oxford and New York: Oxford University Press, 1997).
48 Dialogue with Lee Hsien Loong at the SG50+ Conference, July 2, 2015, transcribed at http://www.pmo.gov.sg/newsroom/transcript-dialogue-prime-minister-lee-hsien-loong-sg50-conference-2-july-2015
49 Randy Martin, *The Financialization of Everyday Life* (Philadelphia: Temple University Press, 2002).
50 Eng Beng Lim, "No Cane, No Gain: Harry, Queer Discipline, and Me," *Bully-Bloggers*, available online at https://bullybloggers.wordpress.com/2015/03/29/no-cane-no-gain-harry-queer-discipline-and-me-by-eng-beng-lim
51 Anna Tsing, "Supply Chains and the Human Condition," *Rethinking Marxism* 21(2), 2007, 148-176.
52 Stefano Harney and Fred Moten, *The Undercommons: Fugitive Planning & Black Study* (Brooklyn: Autonomedia, 2013).
53 For more on Martha Atienza see https://www.singaporebiennale.org/martha-atienza.php; on Hemali Bhuta https://www.singaporebiennale.org/hemali-bhuta.php
54 Denise Ferreira da Silva, *Toward a Global Idea of Race* (Minneapolis, MN: University of Minnesota Press, 2007).
55 Michael Malay, "Buy a discount maid at Singapore's malls," Al Jazeera, 27 June 2014, accessible online at https://www.aljazeera.com/indepth/features/2014/06/buy-discount-maid-at-singapore-malls-201462495012940207.html; and Kirsten Han, "Singapore's migrant workers face abuse and resentment," *Southeast Asia Globe*, April 27, 2016, available online at https://southeastasiaglobe.com/singapore-migrant-workers.
56 James C. Scott, *The Art of Not Being Governed: An Anarchist History of Upland South East Asia* (New Haven, CT: Yale University Press, 2011).
57 *Ibid.*
58 See Carl A. Trocki's crucial book on the colonial history of Singapore and its legacy, *Singapore: Wealth, Power and the Culture of Control* (London: Routledge, 2006).
59 Gayatri Chakravorty Spivak, "Righting Wrongs," *South Atlantic Quarterly* 103(2-3), 2004, 523-81.

INDENT (TO SERVE THE DEBT)

60 We were privileged to hear Professor Lott discuss gradual emancipation at a roundtable she designed and convened at Brown University on April 22, 2015.

61 J. Kameron Carter, "Paratheological Blackness," *The South Atlantic Quarterly* 112:4, Fall 2013, 589-611.

62 Gayle Salamon, *Assuming a Body: Transgender and Rhetorics of Materiality* (New York: Columbia University Press, 2010).

63 Sylvia Wynter, *Maskerade: A 'Jonkunnu' Musical Play*, in Yvonne Brewster, ed., *Mixed Company: Three Early Jamaican Plays* (London: Oberon Books, 2012).

AGAINST MANAGEMENT: WATERMELON MANNISHNESS

64 Marina Vishmidt, *Speculation as a Mode of Production: Forms of Value Subjectivity in Art and Capital* (London: Haymarket Books, 2019).

65 Hortense Spillers, "Mama's Baby, Papa's Maybe: An American Grammar Book," *Diacritics* 17(2), 1987, 64-81.

66 Oscar Zeta Acosta, *The Revolt of the Cockroach People* (New York, NY: Vintage, 1989).

67 Franz Kafka, *Letters to Felice*, Ed. Erich Heller and Jürgen Born. Trans. James Stern and Elizabeth Duckworth (New York: Shocken Books, 1973) 47.

68 Or: Think of it as having an Apple embedded in your back. It is as if one has not only become more and less than one, but also that here, where augmentation and degeneration combine, one becomes hardware.

PLANTOCRACY AND COMMUNISM?

69 This chapter began as a call and response with our friends at BAK Wietske Mass and Maria Hlavajova. See Gerald Raunig, *Dividuum: Machinic Capitalism and Molecular Revolution*, trans. Aileen Derieg (New York: Semiotext[e], 2016) for more on the non-individually derived dividual.

70 See Dionne Brand, *A Map to the Door of No Return: Notes to Belonging* (Toronto: Vintage Canada, 2002) and Toni Morrison, *Beloved* (New York: Vintage, 1987, 2004).

71 Amiri Baraka (LeRoi Jones), "Return of the Native" in William J. Harris, ed. *The LeRoi Jones/Amiri Baraka Reader*, 2nd Edition (New York: Basic Books, 1999) 217 and M. NourbeSe Philip, "Dis Place – The Space Between" in *A Genealogy of Resistance and Other Essays* (Toronto: The Mercury Press, 1997) 74-112.

WHO DETERMINES IF SOMETHING IS HABITABLE?

72 In a different, more elaborate and illuminating way, through a generative encounter she stages between Frankétienne and Édouard Glissant that deepens and exceeds their relation,

Kaiama L. Glover discusses this distinction between showing and telling. See her "Showing vs. Telling: 'Spiralisme' in the Light of 'Antillanité,'" *Journal of Haitian Studies* 14(1), Spring 2008, 91–117, and *Haiti Unbound: A Spiralist Challenge to the Postcolonial Canon* (Liverpool: Liverpool University Press, 2010), 179–237.

73 Quoted in Alan Watts, *In My Own Way: An Autobiography* (Novato, CA: New World Library, 1972), 106.

74 Carolin Wiedemann and Soenke Zehle, "Depletion Design," *Depletion Design: A Glossary of Network Ecologies* (Amsterdam: Institute of Network Cultures, 2012), 5.

75 See Reiner Schürmann, *Heidegger on Being and Acting: From Principles to Anarchy* (Bloomington: Indiana University Press, 1987).

76 See LeRoi Jones, "A contract. (for the destruction and rebuilding of Paterson)," *The Dead Lecturer* (New York: Grove Press, 1964), 10–11; William Carlos Williams, *Paterson* (New York: New Directions, 1995); and Allen Iverson's outline of a theory of practice and the game, accessible online at https://youtu.be/eGDBR2L5kzI.

77 *The Martian*, dir. Ridley Scott (Los Angeles: Twentieth Century Fox, 2015).

78 See Adelita Husni-Bey et al., *Emotional Depletion: An Immigration Lawyer's Handbook* (New York, NY: Adelita Husni-Bey, 2018).

SUICIDE AS A CLASS

79 See George Padmore, *The Life and Struggles of Negro Toilers* (1931), https://www.marxists.org/archive/padmore/1931/negro-toilers/index.htm

80 Martin L. Kilson, *The Transformation of the African American Intelligentsia, 1880-2012* (Cambridge: Harvard University Press, 2014).

THE GIFT OF CORRUPTION

81 Stephen Booth, *Precious Nonsense: The Gettysburg Address, Ben Jonson's Epitaph son His Son, and Twelfth Night* (Berkeley: University of California Press, 1998) 72.

82 Jan Patočka, *Body, Community, Language, World*, trans. Erazim Kohák (Chicago: Open Court, 1998), 178.

83 Robert Duncan, "Towards an Open Universe," James Maynard, ed. *Robert Duncan: Collected Essays and Other Prose* (Berkeley: University of California Press, 2014) 129. Duncan quotes Erwin Schrödinger, *What is Life?* (Cambridge: Cambridge University Press, 2012) 69.

84 Gary Zukav, *The Dancing Wu-Li Masters: An Overview of the New Physics* (New York: HarperOne, 2001) 72. Zukav quotes Werner Heisenberg, *Physics and Philosophy: The Revolution in Modern Science* (New York: Harper & Row, 1962) 41.

www.ingramcontent.com/pod-product-compliance
Ingram Content Group UK Ltd.
Pitfield, Milton Keynes, MK11 3LW, UK
UKHW020332240126
467308UK00002B/3